Neuro-Linguistic Programming Made Easy

Jon Adams

CONTENTS

INTRODUCTION

Welcome to 'Neuro-Linguistic Programming Made Easy', where the complex becomes accessible and self-improvement is at your fingertips. From the outset, this book is designed for those curious about the mind's untapped potential and eager to harness it through the power of NLP. You'll embark on a journey that distills dense psychological theories into clear, actionable insights.

The term 'Neuro-Linguistic Programming' can seem daunting, often cloaked in jargon that can alienate the layperson. However, at its core, NLP is about understanding the language of your mind and rewriting your life's script for the better. This book aims to break down those barriers, offering a straightforward guide to NLP's foundational principles and practical techniques that can be applied in your daily routines.

Expect to learn how to decode your thought patterns, sharpen your communication skills, and cultivate positive change in yourself and your relationships. With concise explanations and relatable examples, 'Neuro-Linguistic Programming Made Easy' promises to illuminate the path of personal growth and empowerment.

Whether your goal is to become more persuasive in your professional life, foster deeper connections with those around you, or simply gain more control over your internal dialogue, this book is a rich resource. By the end, readers will not only understand NLP but will also have the tools to implement its strategies—turning once-abstract concepts into a tangible skill set that enhances every aspect of life. Get ready to explore the transformative power of NLP, presented with ease and clarity.

THE FOUNDATIONS OF NLP

Neuro-Linguistic Programming, commonly referred to as NLP, stands at the intersection of psychology and communication, offering a toolkit for enhancing personal growth and interpersonal interaction. Its primary functions involve understanding and harnessing the power of language and thought patterns to foster positive change and effective communication. Widely recognized for its practical applications, NLP can significantly influence areas such as leadership, therapy, education, and self-help by optimizing the ways in which we perceive and convey information. Through mastering NLP principles, individuals gain heightened self-awareness and a robust skill set to improve various aspects of their personal and professional lives.

Neuro-Linguistic Programming began with the work of Richard Bandler and John Grinder in the 1970s. These two men started by studying the therapeutic methods of successful psychologists and uncovered patterns that seemed to contribute to their effectiveness. From these observations, Bandler and Grinder developed a set of strategies and models.

As NLP has evolved, it has branched out from its origins in therapy to include applications in a broad range of fields such as business, education, and sports. The discipline now encompasses not only the original models but also a variety of tools and techniques aimed at improving communication, personal development, and problem-solving skills.

One of the key tenets of NLP is the idea that language and thought are interconnected and can shape our experience of the world. By changing the way we talk to and about ourselves, NLP suggests we can alter our thoughts and feelings, thus impacting our behavior and the results we achieve in various aspects of life.

Another important aspect is the concept of 'modeling', which involves observing and mapping the successful behaviors and thought patterns of high-achievers to be replicated for similar success. This approach has led to a richer understanding of what contributes to excellence in human performance and provided a framework for others to develop their skills in a structured way.

Today's NLP continues to grow and adapt, integrating new findings from neuroscience and psychology, ensuring its relevance and utility in a fast-changing world. Those practicing NLP use it to facilitate change, enhance communication, and foster personal growth, illustrating the enduring impact of the foundation laid by Bandler and Grinder's initial work.

Let's take a deeper look at the strategies and models created by Richard Bandler and John Grinder that stand as the bedrock of Neuro-Linguistic Programming (NLP). Imagine the early NLP models as the lens of a camera – fine-tuning focus to capture the essence of an exquisite scene. Among these is the Meta-Model, a linguistic tool that sharpens our verbal lens to clarify vague language, much like clarifying a fuzzy image to reveal the vibrant details hidden within.

In the Meta-Model, we have specific components: deletions, distortions, and generalizations, akin to filters that can obscure or alter reality. Deletions in our speech can leave out vital information, just as a photograph cropped too tightly might omit crucial parts of the scene. Distortions can twist our words and thoughts, similar to a funhouse mirror that warps our reflection. Generalizations, meanwhile, are like broad brush strokes in a painting, which can sometimes lose the finer details.

In the practice of NLP, these techniques are used to unpack a client's language, much as a master mechanic might disassemble an engine – piece by piece – to diagnose an issue. With meticulous care, the practitioner explores the client's words to uncover the underlying belief structures and assumptions, enabling them to bring the obscured details of their thought patterns into sharp relief.

When it comes to modeling, it's less about imitation and more about distillation. It involves deconstructing the expertise of high achievers as though their excellence were a complex recipe, and then extracting each ingredient and step to create a blueprint that others can follow. Sensory acuity and behavioral flexibility are the chef's keen senses and nimble fingers, allowing them to adjust seasoning and technique in response to the dish's needs.

Now, fast forward to how these foundational NLP strategies are employed today – for instance, in the business arena. Here, anchoring is like setting a bookmark in a favorite book, allowing a negotiator to return to a state of confidence at will. Reframing, on the other hand, is like changing the frame on a painting, transforming the way a situation is viewed and experienced.

In education, the pacing and leading strategy mirrors the ebb and flow of a dance, where the teacher initially matches the students' rhythm before guiding them to a new tempo and understanding. This creates an environment more conducive to learning, just as a well-choreographed dance yields a more graceful performance.

By understanding these components in detail, we catch a glimpse into the intricate workings of NLP – how it seeks not simply to adjust the external behaviors, but to understand and refine the inner workings of the mind. In embracing these principles, NLP becomes a valuable instrument in our toolkit, providing us with the means to improve the quality of our conversations, our work, and our lives.

Let's think of learning a new sport and how it's a lot like understanding NLP principles. Calibration in NLP is similar to finding your footing in a game. Just as you'd adjust your stance or grip in tennis based on your last swing and how it played out, calibration is about tuning into someone's response to what you say and do, and then tweaking your approach accordingly for better results next time.

Representational systems in NLP are like the different positions players might prefer in a soccer game. Some are visual, preferring to see the field and strategize visually; others are auditory, responding best to the calls of teammates; while kinesthetic players rely on the physical 'feel' of the game. In NLP, we tap into these preferred 'positions' to communicate more effectively.

Finally, the feedback loop can be likened to the immediate rush of knowing if your moves in your sport are working. If your three-pointer swooshes through the basketball net, that's feedback telling you your aim and force was just right. In NLP, feedback loops help us gauge if our communication is having the desired effect, so we can either keep at it or change our tactic — just like tweaking your strategy on the court after missing a shot or scoring a point.

Understanding these principles isn't just a mental exercise; it's about actively using them to improve how we connect with others every day, refining our 'game' of interaction. Keeping these analogies in mind can turn the somewhat abstract concepts of NLP into something we can see, feel, and improve upon just like in any sport we're trying to master.

Here's the breakdown of NLP's representational systems and how they shape our communication and thought processes:

- Visual:
  - Traits: People with a visual style often think in vivid images. It's like having an inner gallery of pictures guiding their thoughts. They may describe scenarios using visual language—imagine someone who speaks as if they're painting a scene with words.
  - Identifying: You can often spot a visual person when they search for the right words, their eyes might wander upwards or to the sides, almost as if they're flipping through a mental photo album to find the images that match their thoughts.
  - Communicating: Engage with them by using descriptive visuals in your language. Think of talking to them as if you're sketching with colorful words, making your storytelling come alive like a comic book strip.

- Auditory:
  - Traits: The auditory folks move to the rhythm of sounds. For them, conversations might feel like a piece of music, where the tone, pitch, and rhythm are just as important as the words themselves.
  - Identifying: They'll really listen to what you're saying, and their eyes might dart sideways as if following a sound wave. They might respond in kind with a voice that rises and falls melodically.
  - Communicating: Speak to them in a way that's rich with auditory texture. It's like being a DJ where your voice can create a soundscape that captures their attention and keeps them tuned in.

- Kinesthetic:
  - Traits: Kinesthetic communicators are the ones who feel their way

through the world. Their language is full of feeling, and they seek physical expressions of communication, such as a handshake or a pat on the back. They're the dancers of conversation, moving with emotion and instinct.

- Identifying: These individuals might look down towards their body as they're speaking, really grounding themselves in their tactile reality. They often speak less of what they see or hear and more about what they feel.

- Communicating: When talking with them, focus on the sensory aspects of your description. Make them feel your words as if they could touch the texture of your language and sense the emotional weight with each sentence.

In a coaching context, understanding these systems allows for a tailored approach. For visual clients, you might use tools like vision boards. With auditory individuals, engage in storytelling and listen intently to their word choices. For kinesthetic clients, incorporate activities that let them physically move or touch objects related to their goals.

Integrating these varied communication methods enhances interactions exponentially. It's like knowing the secret spice blend in a recipe that makes a good dish great. By being attuned to and using these representational systems, conversations can become not only more effective but can resonate on a deeper, more personal level. This is true in personal relationships just as much as it is in professional environments, fostering a sense of connection and understanding across all areas of life.

Establishing rapport is much like tuning into a radio frequency—both require finding the right wavelength for clear communication. In personal interactions, this means listening actively and aligning with the other person's body language and tone of voice, effectively syncing up with their 'broadcast' to ensure the message comes through loud and clear. In the realm of business, rapport creates a channel for smooth, effective exchanges where proposals and negotiations flow more freely, mirroring the ease of listening to a strong signal on the radio. Mastery of this skill can transform relationships, making interactions more rewarding, cooperative, and productive. Connecting with someone's 'frequency' not only conveys that their message is being received, but also that their thoughts and feelings are acknowledged, establishing a mutual trust that is essential for any successful relationship.

Establishing rapport step-by-step can be seen as fine-tuning your interpersonal skills to achieve clear and effective communication:

Step 1: Begin with Open Body Language
Start interactions with an approachable stance. Just like an open radio signal invites listeners, make sure your arms are uncrossed and maintain a relaxed posture to invite conversation and signal willingness to engage.

Step 2: Mirror Gestures Subtly
As the discussion progresses, occasionally match the other person's gestures and postures. This is akin to syncing your frequency to theirs, helping to create a sense of similarity and comfort without imitating or mocking, which can result in a disconnect.

Step 3: Match Tonality and Pacing
Observe the pitch and speed of the other person's speech. Gradually adjust your vocal quality and speech rate to theirs, creating a harmonious dialogue. Imagine trying to harmonize in a duet, where matching your partner's note creates a pleasing resonance.

Step 4: Reflect Vocabulary and Speech Patterns
Pay close attention to the other person's choice of words and phraseology. Incorporate similar language into your responses as a sign that you are on the same wavelength and fully engaged in the exchange.

Step 5: Actively Listen and Provide Feedback
Listen intently to the content of their message as well as the emotions behind it. Then offer feedback that shows your comprehensive understanding, such as nodding in agreement or summarizing their points, ensuring the 'signal' of your communication is received clearly.

Step 6: Maintain the Connection
Keep these techniques consistent throughout your interactions to build and maintain a clear channel of communication. Regularly check in with the other person's reception, asking for their input and perspectives to foster a dynamic and balanced conversation.

Remember, the goal is to establish a connection that makes both parties feel understood and valued, strengthening the rapport over time. Whether in personal affairs or business engagements, mastery of these steps can result in more meaningful, trusting, and fruitful relationships.

Representational systems in NLP are akin to how we each have our favorite streaming service, based on what kind of content resonates with us most. Just like someone might prefer Netflix for its wide range of dramas and documentaries appealing to their visual senses, another person might choose Spotify for the auditory delight of music and podcasts. Similarly, in NLP, some people are visual learners and communicate best through images, diagrams, and mental 'movies.' Others are auditory, favoring spoken word and sounds, and some are kinesthetic, who focus on the emotions and tangible feelings of a conversation. Just as choosing the right streaming service can greatly enhance your entertainment experience, understanding and engaging with a person's preferred representational system significantly improves the quality and depth of communication. Each system, like each platform, offers a unique way to process and enjoy content, tailoring the experience to individual likes and needs, underscoring the importance of personalization in both digital media and interpersonal interactions.

Let's take a deeper look at the nuanced language and techniques within each NLP representational system. Inside the visual system, it's not just about preferring pictures; it's about how images dominate someone's thinking and speaking. When a person says 'see what I mean,' they're often literally visualizing their point. When they suggest looking at an issue 'from another angle,' they're practically turning a situation around in their mental space to examine it from different perspectives—much like a photographer alters angles to capture the essence of a scene.

Moving on to the auditory system, it's more nuanced than just the act of hearing. For those who often say 'sounds good to me,' they're tuning into the verbal aspect of the conversation as if adjusting an equalizer to get the perfect audio balance. When a person says 'that clicks,' they're expressing a moment of clarity much like a musician finding the perfect pitch and rhythm that resonates within them.

As for kinesthetic communicators, their language is rich with tactile and emotive references. Phrases like 'get a handle on it' suggest a desire to grasp something physically as well as mentally, while saying 'solid understanding' conveys a sense of a concept being tangible and real to them—akin to a sculptor feeling the texture of the clay taking shape beneath their fingers.

Grasping these subtle cues allows for communication that's tailored to the listener's internal world, creating deeper understanding and forging stronger connections. It's about harmonizing your message with the listener's preferred channel, like tuning an instrument to the orchestra's pitch—whether in casual conversation or in a more structured professional context. Knowing how to identify and adapt to these representational systems offers precision in interactions, resulting in more effective and fulfilling exchanges that resonate on a personal level.

The process of goal setting in NLP can be likened to the detailed planning of an eagerly anticipated vacation. Think of deciding on your destination as setting your ultimate goal – it's the exciting place you really want to visit. Then, you start planning your itinerary, akin to laying out the specific objectives you'll need to achieve along the way, much like the stops you'd plan to enjoy various attractions. Each reservation you make is like the smaller milestones you'd set – from booking your flights and accommodations to securing tickets to events. These steps entail visualizing the experiences you want to have, essentially programming your expectation of the upcoming journey. Ensuring every detail aligns with your vision of the perfect getaway mirrors how NLP encourages setting goals that resonate deeply with your personal values and beliefs. It's all about crafting a clear, step-by-step map that navigates you through each stage of your journey, leading to an experience that's not only memorable but truly transformative. This careful approach ensures that when the day of departure arrives, you are fully prepared and can enjoy the trip with ease and excitement, just as well-set goals in life empower you to move forward with confidence and anticipation.

Here is the breakdown of the NLP goal-setting process, similar to planning the ideal vacation that's memorable and invigorating:

- **Establishing the Outcome:**
    - **Clearly defining the result you want to achieve:** Just like choosing a vacation spot, you decide on a desired outcome that excites and motivates you.
    - **Ensuring the goal is congruent with personal values:** The destination should be somewhere you'll love, aligning with what you enjoy and believe in, like picking a beach getaway because you value relaxation and sunshine.
    - **Visualizing the achievement of the goal to enhance motivation:** Imagine walking on the beach, like feeling the success of your goal in

advance, to boost your motivation.

- **Identifying Resources:**
- **Leveraging existing skills and knowledge:** Use what you know about traveling to plan the best trip, much like using your skills to achieve your goal.
- **Recognizing external tools or individuals that can aid in the pursuit of the goal:** Just as you might use a travel website or consult a friend who's been to the destination before, identify tools and people that can help.
- **Gathering new resources if gaps are identified:** If you've never been snorkeling, you'd learn or get a guide, just as you'd seek new knowledge for your goal.

- **Creating an Action Plan:**
- **Setting a sequence of specific, actionable steps:** List out each step, from booking your flight to packing your bags, just as you'd outline the steps to reach your goal.
- **Applying timelines to each task to maintain momentum:** Plan when to book tickets or get vaccinations, much like setting timelines for goal milestones.
- **Anticipating potential obstacles and planning contingencies:** If a flight gets canceled, have a backup plan, similar to anticipating challenges in goal achievement.

- **Evaluating Impact:**
- **Reflecting on how achieving the goal will affect personal growth:** Consider how the trip will broaden your horizons, similar to how accomplishing your goal will impact your personal development.
- **Considering the influence on immediate social circles and broader context:** Your vacation stories will impact your friends and family, just as achieving your goal will influence those around you.

- **Continuous Feedback and Adjustment:**
- **Regularly reviewing progress towards the goal:** It's like checking your trip itinerary regularly to ensure everything's on track.
- **Being willing to adjust actions or objectives based on feedback:** If you learn about a must-see spot, you might change your plans; similarly, be open to adjusting your goal path.

- **<u>Finalization and Celebration:</u>**
- **<u>Recognizing the accomplishment of subgoals:</u>** Every excursion on your trip is a mini-celebration, akin to celebrating the small wins on the way to your larger goal.
- **<u>Celebrating the achievement of the main goal to reinforce successful behavior:</u>** Finally reaching your dream destination and reflecting on the journey is as important as celebrating the full achievement of your goal.

Each step of this process is crucial, and like in travel, the joy is as much in the journey as in the destination. Mapping your path to a goal can be as fulfilling as planning the trip of a lifetime, and the experiences gained are treasures of their own.

Developing sensory acuity in NLP is not unlike honing the eye of an artist; both processes involve an increased sensitivity to the finer details. An artist meticulously observes the play of light and shadow, the subtle changes in color, and the texture of their materials. They adjust their technique, sometimes stroke by stroke, to capture the essence of their subject accurately. Similarly, someone skilled in sensory acuity pays close attention to the almost imperceptible shifts in a person's tone of voice, the minute twitches in facial expression, and the slight alterations in body language. Just as an artist uses their refined perception to guide their hand, an individual uses sensory acuity to adjust their responses and communication in real-time. This attention to detail can significantly influence the effectiveness of the interaction, just as the details in a painting can change its overall impact and message.

To develop sensory acuity within NLP, think of yourself as an artist learning to refine their perception of the world. Here's how to sharpen your senses, step by step:

Start by observing baseline behaviors. This is like an artist understanding their basic materials and what they can do. Pay attention to a person's typical posture, usual gestures, and the characteristic patterns in their voice. Notice how they stand when they're relaxed, the hand movements they make when they're excited, and the pace at which they speak when they're comfortable.

Next, look for micro-expressions. Train your eyes to catch quick facial movements that can indicate someone's true feelings. This is similar to an artist capturing the fleeting effects of light. Learn to differentiate genuine smiles from polite ones and pick up on the furrowing of brows that happens in a moment of confusion.

Attune yourself to voice modulations. Focus on the pitch, pace, and volume of someone's speech, much like distinguishing notes in music. Recognize the frustration in a slightly raised voice or the excitement in quickened speech, just as a musician identifies emotion in a song.

Recognize physiological changes. This is about noticing the subtler signs that someone's emotional state has shifted. You might see a change in breathing patterns when someone is nervous or a rapid shift in skin color when they're angry, similar to how an artist might notice a change in light or texture.

Enhance kinesthetic awareness, becoming aware of the energy in a person's body. Feel the tension in their stance or the relaxation in their movements, akin to an artist touching the canvas to feel the texture of the paint.

Commit to practicing and refining these sensory skills. Engage in activities that challenge your perception, like drawing or listening intently to music. Then, review your interactions to see how accurate you were in your observations.

Finally, apply this sensory acuity in your communication. Use your awareness to connect with others more deeply. Adjust your manner of speaking or your own body language to better align with others, much like an artist might revise their painting to convey the right emotion.

Through each step, remember you're learning to play a symphony of human interaction with the finesse of a consummate artist. Each sensory observation is a note in the melody of connection, and as you master them, your ability to communicate and connect will grow richer and more resonant.

Tony Robbins, a notable figure in personal development, employs NLP techniques similar to strategies that drive success in businesses and sports coaching. Just as a coach might analyze game footage to perfect an athlete's technique, Robbins scrutinizes behavioral patterns to enhance personal and professional performance. He uses goal-setting and motivational strategies akin to a business setting targets and rallying its team, focusing on measurable outcomes and consistent feedback.

In his seminars, Robbins might direct an audience to visualize achieving their goals, which is not unlike how a visualization exercise before a big game can prime an athlete's mental state for peak performance. He also employs linguistic flexibility, echoing the way effective leaders communicate, adapting their message to resonate best with their audience, whether it be employees, customers, or stakeholders.

Both in high-powered boardrooms and on championship-winning teams, the principles of clear communication, strategic planning, and maintaining a growth mindset are critical. Robbins leverages these same principles in his work, demonstrating how NLP can unlock potential and foster success across a variety of fields by cultivating strong mental foundations and clarity of intent.

Let's take a deeper look at the precision of NLP strategies Tony Robbins employs, much like a master craftsman employing tools to sculpt a masterpiece:

- **Precise Goal-Setting Techniques:**
    - Robbins meticulously defines clear goals in high definition, asking probing questions that clarify not just what clients want to achieve, but why it matters to them, akin to setting a GPS with a specific destination and purpose for the journey.
    - His criteria for creating actionable objectives are akin to a chef's recipe—a list of ingredients and steps that, when combined, create a desired dish. Each objective must be specific, measurable, attainable, relevant, and timely (SMART).

- **Visualization Practices:**
    - Robbins advocates for a step-by-step process of mental visualization that begins with closing your eyes and painting the goal in your mind with rich detail, similar to an architect envisioning a building before the first brick is laid.

- He encourages the use of sensory-rich language, urging you to hear the applause, see the success, feel the excitement—immersing all senses as if you're already living the desired outcome.

- **<u>Adaptive Linguistic Techniques:</u>**
- Analyzing Robbins' language patterns is like decoding a powerful speech; he uses metaphors and analogies to relate complex ideas to his audience's experiences, making concepts as relatable as a neighbor explaining how to plant a garden.
- His strategies for addressing different audience communication styles reflect the adaptability of a chameleon, changing his linguistic approach to match the mood and engagement level of his listeners.

- **<u>Method for Evaluating Performance and Progress:</u>**
- Robbins' techniques for measuring personal growth include establishing metrics that are as tangible as a runner's time improvements lap by lap on a track.
- These evaluations inform strategy adjustments, similar to a pilot altering course based on weather radar feedback to ensure a smooth flight.

- **<u>Framework for Feedback Integration:</u>**
- Robbins has developed a system for feedback that's as comprehensive as a 360-degree review in a corporate setting, soliciting perspectives from all angles to paint a full picture of where you stand.
- This feedback then directly informs the refinement of goals or communication, as a craftsman would sand down a rough edge upon review to ensure the finished product is flawless.

In dissecting Robbins' use of these strategies, we see a reflection of fundamental principles applied in the pinnacle of business and sports leadership. These principles arm individuals with a toolset for excellence, positioning them to navigate the complexities of their endeavors with the agility and foresight of elite performers in any arena.

Consider the principles of Neuro-Linguistic Programming (NLP) as foundational tools for personal development; they are designed to increase your self-awareness and enhance your communication skills. Understanding NLP concepts, such as representational systems and the use of language patterns, can significantly improve your ability to connect with others. These techniques can also function as a blueprint for personal transformation, offering structured approaches to reframe thoughts and behaviors that no longer serve you. By learning and applying the practices of NLP, you can pave a pathway to a more fulfilling life, marked by improved personal relationships and a clear sense of purpose. So reflect on how integrating NLP strategies into your daily life could serve as a catalyst for positive change and contribute to your overall growth.

BUILDING RAPPORT THE HEART OF NLP

Rapport is a fundamental element within the framework of Neuro-Linguistic Programming (NLP), serving as a key to successful communication. It involves establishing a connection with others that is characterized by mutual understanding and responsiveness. This connection is crucial for creating an environment where ideas can be exchanged freely and objectives can be achieved more effectively. In practice, rapport is about attuning to the person you are communicating with by matching their body language, tone, and verbal patterns to create a sense of alignment and harmony. The benefits of such synchronization are tangible: it fosters trust, breaks down barriers, and facilitates the openness necessary for productive dialogue and influence. By building rapport, individuals can navigate conversations more skillfully, leading to better outcomes in personal relationships, business negotiations, and therapeutic settings.

Let's unpack the application of rapport techniques in NLP with the precision of a jeweler setting delicate stones, each step critical to the integrity of the final piece.

- **<u>Breakdown of Rapport Techniques:</u>**
- **<u>Verbal and Non-Verbal Cues:</u>**
  - Observe the rhythm of the other person's speech—is it fast like a lively tennis rally, or more measured like a leisurely game of catch? Match their tempo.
  - Notice posture: are they sitting back relaxed, hands folded calmly like resting on a Sunday porch, or leaning forward with hands animated as if reaching for an exciting new novel on a shelf? Adopt a similar stance.
- **<u>Mirroring Practice:</u>**
  - Start with simple mirroring, like a shadow following on a sunny afternoon walk, initially reflecting small gestures before progressing to more significant postures and expressions.
  - Avoid mimicry; instead, allow your actions to be a gentle, natural response, subtly mirroring as if your movements are in a dance, following the lead of your partner.
- **<u>Gauging Success:</u>**
  - Observe their reactions as clues to the success of your rapport, like checking the temperature of the water before a swim. Look for smiles, nods,

or a more relaxed demeanor as signs of successful rapport.

- If you sense resistance, like a shift in wind direction, adjust your approach smoothly without losing stride, as a skilled sailor tacks in changing winds.

- <u>Practical Application in Various Contexts:</u>
- <u>In Personal Relationships:</u>

- Map out the conversation, recognizing and steering away from conversational icebergs—topics or habits that might cool down the warmth of rapport.

- Emphasize active listening; make sure to hear and affirm the other's feelings like recognizing the individual notes in a beloved song.

- <u>In Professional Settings:</u>

- During negotiations, mirror to build rapport but maintain your grounding like a tree with deep roots—solid and unmoved by the gusts of differing opinions.

- In leadership, use rapport to create a group cadence, much like a drummer sets the beat for a band, leading to synchronization and harmony.

- <u>In Therapeutic Environments:</u>

- Therapists can build rapport by mirroring to show empathy, like reflecting the warmth of the sun back onto someone who's been in the shade.

- Pay close attention to the client's pacing and emotional state, providing a verbal and non-verbal safe haven that invites openness and healing.

Through these meticulous and thoughtful applications of rapport techniques, the mastery of communication in NLP is revealed—not only in the mechanics of the practice but in the subtle harmonies it creates, drawing individuals closer to a shared tune of understanding and connection.

Building rapport through techniques such as mirroring and matching can be likened to the act of walking in step with a friend. Just as you naturally adjust your stride to match their pace, creating a comfortable and synchronized rhythm, mirroring involves adjusting your body language, tone, and speech patterns to resonate with the person you're communicating with. This doesn't mean copying their every move, which can feel intrusive, but rather subtly reflecting elements of their behavior, like nodding when they nod or smiling when they smile. Matching, on the other hand, involves speaking at a similar pace or using a vocabulary that aligns with theirs, similar to using the same walking speed or taking the same size steps as your friend. The aim is to create a feeling of affinity and connectedness, making the other person feel understood and at ease, paving the way for a more open and fruitful exchange of ideas.

Here is the breakdown of mirroring and matching techniques, essential tools in the rapport-builder's toolbox that help create a bridge of understanding and trust in communication:

- **Mirroring Techniques:**
  - **Facial Expressions:**
    - **Smiling:** Reflect a genuine smile in friendly settings as naturally as sharing the warmth of the sun.
    - **Concern:** Mirror expressions of concern in serious discussions, showing empathy like offering a comforting blanket on a chilly evening.
  - **Body Language:**
    - **Open Postures:** Adopt open gestures that invite conversation, as if opening your doors for a welcome guest.
    - **Hand Gestures:** Use hand movements that echo the other person's to underscore shared points, like musicians playing in harmony.
    - **Head Movements:** Nod in agreement to show understanding, as simple as tapping your foot to the rhythm of a familiar tune.
  - **Vocal Characteristics:**
    - **Pitch and Pace:** Match the pitch and pace of your conversation partner subtly, like adjusting your stride when walking side by side.
    - **Volume:** Keep your speaking volume at a level akin to theirs, creating a balanced auditory space as if tuning two instruments to the same note.

- **Matching Techniques:**
  - **Lexical Choice:**
    - Identify words and phrases that the other person uses and weave them into your responses, as if sprinkling their favorite spices into a shared meal.
  - **Conversational Pacing:**
    - Adjust the rhythm and speed of your own speech to align with theirs, fostering a conversational dance that feels in step and effortless.

- **Assessing Alignment:**
  - Watch for signs of a stronger connection, such as more lively back-and-forth exchanges or a relaxed atmosphere, indicating the efficacy of your mirroring, much like seeing a reflection come into focus.
  - If you detect discomfort or disengagement, recalibrate your approach as smoothly as a chef adjusts a recipe, seeking the perfect blend of flavors.

By understanding and applying these nuanced techniques, one can navigate the subtle currents of conversation, guiding interactions towards mutual understanding and meaningful connections, just as a skilled host intuitively ensures the comfort and engagement of their guests.

At the heart of building rapport lies the psychological concepts of empathy and trust. Empathy is our ability to understand and share the feelings of another — think of it as getting into someone else's shoes, not just to stand there, but to walk around in them. It's how we tune in to what others are feeling and reflect that understanding back to them. Trust, on the other hand, is the firm belief in the reliability or truth of someone — it's the glue that holds human interactions together. You could compare it to the confidence you place in a bridge you cross; the stronger it is, the more easily you tread. When empathy and trust are present in interactions, they fertilize the ground for rapport to grow. They create a safe space for openness, much like the warm environment of a greenhouse allows plants to thrive. Together, these elements form the foundation upon which rapport is built, enabling genuine connection and smooth communication.

Building rapport relies heavily on fostering empathy and trust. Here's how you can cultivate these essential components in any context:

- **Fostering Empathy:**
  - **Active Listening:**
    - Focus fully on the speaker, putting aside distractions.
    - Maintain eye contact to show you are engaged.
    - Nod and provide verbal affirmations like "I see" or "I understand."
    - Paraphrase their words to confirm understanding, asking questions like "What I'm hearing is..." or "Do you mean that...?"
  - **Validation:**
    - Acknowledge their feelings with statements such as "It makes sense you'd feel that way given the situation."
    - Avoid judgment and criticism; aim to be open and accepting of their emotional experience.
  - **Emotional Sharing:**
    - Share your own emotions when appropriate to show empathy, using phrases like "I felt similar when..." to establish a reciprocal emotional understanding.

- **Building Trust:**

- **Consistency:**
- Be reliable in your actions and follow through on promises, showing that others can depend on you over time.
- Stick to routines or agreements established within relationships, like always calling when you say you will.
- **Confidentiality:**
- Keep sensitive information private, reinforcing that you are a safe person to confide in.
- Reinforce this by saying, "I want you to know you can trust me with this."
- **Support:**
- Show unwavering support in your words and actions, like backing up a colleague's idea in a meeting or standing by a friend's decision.

- **Measuring Rapport:**
- **Feedback:**
- Ask for feedback on your interaction, using questions like "How are we doing on this project?" or "Is there anything more I can do to help?"
- Pay attention to non-verbal signals indicating trust and comfort, such as relaxed posture and open facial expressions.
- **Adapting:**
- If feedback indicates disconnect, adapt by analyzing which behaviors may have contributed to the issue and modifying them, whether it means changing the way you provide feedback or making more time for listening.

By systematically applying these strategies, you can improve how you connect with others, ultimately enhancing your personal and professional relationships. The key is to practice consistently, be mindful of the reactions you receive, and adjust accordingly to pave the way toward stronger rapport.

Public figures like Oprah Winfrey and Barack Obama have mastered the art of rapport-building, turning interviews and speeches from mere formalities into deep, engaging connections. Oprah's interview technique is a masterclass in empathy—she listens with an intensity that makes the interviewee feel like the only person in the world, as if they're sharing secrets over a kitchen table. She mirrors emotions with her expressions, nods, and words, creating a space that feels safe and understood, enabling her guests to open up as they would to a long-time confidant.

Barack Obama's public speaking, on the other hand, utilizes trust to create rapport with his audience. Like a skilled captain who navigates a ship through waves, he acknowledges his audience's concerns and speaks to their experiences, bringing everyone on board with his vision. His consistent use of inclusive language and collective pronouns weaves individual listeners into a shared narrative, fostering a sense of unity and personal connection.

These techniques exemplify how rapport-building can elevate communication from transactional exchanges to transformative interactions. By employing such strategies, these figures have turned their platforms into spaces of meaningful dialogue, demonstrating the power of rapport in any context.

Let's take a closer look at the nuanced communication tactics employed by Oprah Winfrey and Barack Obama to connect with their audiences in a meaningful way:

- **<u>Oprah Winfrey's Interview Strategies:</u>**
  - **<u>Active Listening:</u>** Oprah engages with her guests by exercising active listening. She maintains sincere eye contact as if each person's story is a captivating movie, and she's absorbed in every frame. Her knack for paraphrasing, repeating back what her guests have said in her own words, like a poet finding a new rhyme for an old verse, ensures mutual understanding and validates their experiences.
  - **<u>Emotional Calibration:</u>** She tunes her emotions with precision, mirroring the emotional undertones of her guests' narratives. If a guest shares a moment of joy, her genuine smile amplifies it, just as sunlight brightens a room. When faced with sorrow, her demeanor softens, as though offering a gentle hand-hold through difficult memories.
  - **<u>Open-Ended Questions:</u>** With a skill akin to a gardener nurturing seedlings, Oprah uses open-ended questions to encourage her guests to unfold richer, more detailed accounts of their lives, prompting an exploration of the soil of their experiences rather than just the surface.

- **<u>Barack Obama's Public Speaking Tactics:</u>**
  - **<u>Inclusive Addressing:</u>** Barack Obama approaches diverse audiences by tailoring his message like a tailor adjusts a suit for the perfect fit, ensuring everyone feels included and understood.
  - **<u>Storytelling:</u>** He weaves stories into his oratory, making points relatable as familiar landmarks on a well-traveled road, inviting listeners along on a shared journey of understanding.

- **<u>Verbal Cues and Techniques:</u>** In his speeches, Obama's careful selection of words and the rhythm of his pacing serve to build trust as reliably as the consistent heartbeat of a favorite song engenders relaxation and joy. The pace, inflections, and choice of language are like musical notes that resonate within the collective heart of his audience.

By studying these finely honed techniques of two master communicators, readers can gain insights into how to create rapport themselves. These examples demonstrate that rapport isn't just about the words we say but how we say them and the genuine connections we forge using the language of empathy and trust.

To assess past interactions for successful rapport building, approach it with the analytical mindset of a sports coach reviewing game footage. Begin by recalling the conversation in detail, replaying key moments in your mind. Focus on moments of engagement: were there nods, smiles, and verbal acknowledgments that indicated a strong connection? Consider the ease of the interaction: was there a back-and-forth exchange akin to a ball smoothly passed between teammates?

Then, identify areas for improvement. Reflect on any moments of disconnect or discomfort, perhaps where the conversation stalled or became one-sided, much like plays that didn't go as planned on the field. Did you perhaps talk over the other person or fail to pick up on cues that they wanted to say more? Analyzing these scenarios provides invaluable insight into how your communication can be adapted and improved for future interactions.

In doing so, you're not just looking for what went wrong but also what went right. Solidify those successful strategies in your playbook for the next time. By consistently reviewing your interactions with a critical eye, you can develop a sharper sense of how to foster rapport, making every conversation an opportunity to hone your skills.

Here is the breakdown of steps to review and evaluate your past conversations to enhance rapport-building skills, much like a gardener tends to plants, ensuring each has the right conditions to flourish:

- **<u>Review Process:</u>**
  - **<u>Replay Interaction:</u>**

- Observe instances of eye contact: Solid eye contact is like the sun for plants—necessary for growth.

- Notice nodding: Just as plants bend towards the light, nodding shows you are leaning into the conversation.

- Recognize active participation: Both parties should contribute like a duet harmonizing in a melody.

- **Emotional Response:**

- Identify smiles: A smile in conversation is like rain on soil, refreshing and nurturing the interaction.

- Listen for laughter: It acts as sunlight breaking through clouds, brightening the atmosphere.

- Observe open body language: Open arms are like open petals; they signal receptivity and welcome.

- **Flow of Conversation:**

- Detect a natural pace: Assurance in the conversation's tempo is like a steady stream that flows effortlessly.

- Sense tension or stagnation: Halted conversation is like overwatered soil—too much in one place can suffocate growth.

- **Improvement Identification:**

- **Missteps:**

- Trace misunderstandings: Unearth the root of the issue as you would a weed, to prevent future occurrences.

- **Missed Opportunities:**

- Highlight times when deeper questions or empathy were called for, akin to providing nutrients to soil.

- **Interruptions:**

- Note instances of interruption, which are disruptive like sudden storms are to a garden.

- **Strategy Development:**

- **Positive Reinforcement:**

- Keep conducive practices: What nourished the conversation? Those are like the successful conditions you want to replicate.

- **Behavior Adjustment:**

- Decide on new methods: Adjust as needed, just as you might relocate a plant to a sunnier spot.

- **Implementation for Improvement:**

- **Practice:**

- Engage in exercises: Role-play or mindfulness to become more attuned to conversational dynamics.
   - **Feedback Loop:**
   - Seek feedback: Just as a plant grows towards the light, orient yourself towards constructive criticism to better your rapport-building skills.

By methodically nurturing your communication skills through introspection and active improvement, you can cultivate a thriving garden of interactions marked by strong rapport, trust, and mutual respect.

To weave rapport-building techniques into your everyday interactions, consider it akin to following a tried-and-true recipe when cooking a favorite dish. Begin with the base: active listening. Just as you would start with quality ingredients, give your full attention to the person you're speaking with, ensuring they feel valued and heard. Next, add a pinch of empathy to the mixture by acknowledging their feelings and perspectives, like adding salt to enhance the flavors.

Stir in body language mirroring gently, as you might fold in eggs into a batter, subtly aligning your posture and gestures with theirs to create harmony. Sprinkle in matching speech patterns—maintaining a similar tone, pace, and volume—much like seasoning to taste.

Finally, garnish your interaction with open-ended questions, encouraging the sharing of thoughts and experiences, just as you might finish a dish with a sprig of fresh herbs for presentation and added flavor. By combining these elements thoughtfully and with care, you can nurture a rapport as satisfying and rewarding as a beautifully executed meal shared with friends. Remember, the key to both is being attentive and responsive to the process and the needs of those you're engaged with.

Let's take a closer look at the key ingredients in the recipe for rapport-building and how to blend them seamlessly into everyday interactions:

- **Steps for Active Listening:**
   - Imagine your mind as a stage where the speaker is the spotlighted solo performer. Clear away personal thoughts and mental clutter like unnecessary props so that the speaker's message is front and center.
   - Think of nods and eye contact as applause, signaling to the speaker that

their performance—their message—is resonating with the audience, which is you.

- When you repeat or rephrase their words, it's similar to playing back a recording for clarity, ensuring the message was captured correctly.

- Techniques to Express Empathy:

- Pay attention to the speaker's emotions as if you were reading a book, looking for descriptions of feelings that help you understand the character better.

- Share a bit of your own story when it matches the theme of theirs, but keep it brief, like a footnote that supports the main text but doesn't overshadow it.

- Body Language Mirroring:

- Observe their gestures and stances as if you were a painter capturing their essence on canvas, and reflect that essence in your own 'artwork' of body language—but subtly enough that it doesn't become an imitation.

- Practice mirroring in low-stakes environments, such as casual conversations, to hone this skill so when it's needed, it flows naturally like a gentle brushstroke.

- Matching Speech Patterns:

- Tune your ear to the speaker's vocal pitch and pacing as if you were adjusting the frequency on a radio to match their station's signal.

- Reflect the tone and emotional content of the conversation in your own speech, using modulation of your voice to harmonize with theirs.

- Utilizing Open-Ended "Questions:

- Craft your questions to be gateways to deeper insights, much like opening a door to a room full of possibilities rather than a yes/no question which is like peering through a keyhole.

- Follow their narrative with gentle probes, as if watering a plant, enough to nourish it and encourage growth without overwhelming it.

By weaving these actions into your communication style, rapport-building becomes an intuitive part of your social interactions, enriching them and deepening your connections, just as the right mix of ingredients can turn a simple meal into a feast for the senses.

In conclusion, rapport is the linchpin of successful Neuro-Linguistic Programming, facilitating communication that goes beyond the surface to foster genuine human connections. Its effective application has the power to not just improve, but transform personal and professional relationships. Through rapport, we can build bridges of understanding, tailor our communications to individual needs, and create environments where trust and cooperation thrive. As we close this chapter, let us recognize rapport not merely as a concept, but as a pivotal tool, one that when used with skill and sensitivity, has profound implications for the way we connect, communicate, and collaborate with others in every facet of life.

REPRESENTATIONAL SYSTEMS DECODING SENSES

Welcome to the study of representational systems, the mechanisms by which our brains interpret and give meaning to the sensory information we receive from the world around us. Representational systems are the filters through which we perceive sights, sounds, textures, tastes, and smells; they shape our thoughts, memories, and actions. Understanding these systems is essential because they influence every aspect of how we interact with our environment and with others. This chapter will explore the primary functions of these systems in detail, shedding light on their profound impact on communication, behavior, and cognitive processes, providing you with a foundational comprehension of their role in constructing our experiences.

Representational systems are categories our brains use to organize sensory input and give it meaning. There are primarily three: visual, auditory, and kinesthetic. The visual system relates to how we see and visualize, the auditory system to how we hear and speak, and the kinesthetic system to how we feel both physically and emotionally. Each system processes information differently, affecting how we learn, recall experiences, and communicate. When we understand and recognize these systems in ourselves and others, it enhances our ability to convey and interpret messages effectively. For instance, a person with a primary visual representational system might say, "I see what you mean," while an auditory person might say, "That sounds right to me." Recognizing these patterns can help us tailor our communication to better connect with others, improving interactions in both personal and professional settings. This knowledge equips us with the insight to understand our mental processing on a deeper level, letting us harness our strengths and address our weaknesses more systematically.

The visual system operates akin to a sophisticated camera within our minds, transforming light and shapes into images that we understand and recognize. When a painter or graphic designer selects specific colors and forms, they're not just creating something visually appealing—they're effectively communicating through a visual language that can evoke emotions or actions in the viewer. For example, an advertisement may use bold reds and stark contrasts to grab attention and provoke urgency, much as a stop sign commands drivers to halt.

In the auditory system, the brain interprets sound frequencies in a manner somewhat like an audio equalizer. Musicians and sound engineers work with these frequencies, adjusting pitch and volume to create auditory textures and narratives. Just as a finely tuned guitar string can deliver a clear, resonant note, a skilled musician can play with sound frequencies to elicit specific emotional responses from their audience, such as a sense of calm with soft, mellow tones or excitement with upbeat, vibrant rhythms.

The kinesthetic system synthesizes physical sensations and emotional feelings, serving as the body's internal sense of position and movement. Athletes and dancers, for instance, rely heavily on this system, sensing the exact positioning of their limbs and the subtleties in their muscles to execute precise and graceful movements. This is not unlike the way a ship's captain must sense and respond to the ocean's currents or an airplane pilot must remain attuned to airspeed and altitude, each actor using sensory feedback to maintain balance, control, and optimal performance.

Understanding these representational systems, individuals and professionals can leverage them in diverse contexts. Educators can apply this knowledge to create visual, auditory, or kinesthetic learning experiences tailored to students' needs. Therapists can use these systems to connect with clients, identifying their dominant system to guide conversations and interventions. In art, knowledge of these systems allows for more impactful expression, while in corporate settings, this understanding can improve communication, leading to better collaboration and productivity. Recognizing and adapting to the primary representational systems of ourselves and those around us thus serves as a powerful tool, refining our approach to learning, creativity, and interpersonal connection.

Just as a camera lens focuses light to capture a snapshot, our visual system uses the eye's lens to gather light and shape it into the images we see. The retina, like camera film or a digital sensor, records these light patterns, while the brain develops this raw data into the vibrant colors and motion of our conscious view, not unlike the post-processing that turns a raw photograph into a stunning picture. But it's not only about capturing what's in front of us—our visual system also interprets these images, giving context and meaning, similar to how a photographer chooses a frame to tell a story. This complex yet elegant process is the crux of how we navigate our world, recognize faces, and appreciate sunsets, playing a vital role in our interactions and memories.

Here is the breakdown on how our visual system captures and interprets an image, explained through familiar analogies to simplify this intricate process:

- **<u>Components of the Eye:</u>**
  - **<u>Cornea and Lens:</u>**
  - Think of them as the camera's autofocus, bending light to sharpen the image, ensuring that what hits the retina is clear and precise.
  - **<u>Retina:</u>**
  - The retina acts like a high-definition sensor, with rods and cones as the pixels. Rods are specialists in low-light scenarios, while cones handle the vibrant panorama of colors in daylight.
  - **<u>Optic Nerve:</u>**
  - Picture the optic nerve as a high-speed data cable, transmitting the intricate details captured by the eye's 'sensor' to the 'computer' that is the brain.

- **<u>Image Processing in the Brain:</u>**
  - **<u>Visual Cortex:</u>**
  - The visual cortex is the photo editor, rendering signals from the eye into images, adding depth and movement to create the final picture we 'see'.
  - **<u>Association Areas:</u>**
  - Association areas serve as the memory bank, sorting through past experiences and contexts to ascribe meaning to the visual data, similar to tagging photos for future retrieval.

- **<u>Practical Application:</u>**
  - **<u>Lighting Conditions:</u>**
  - Just as photographers adjust shutter speed and aperture according to light, our eyes adapt to brightness and shadows, affecting how the world appears to us.
  - **<u>Occupational Significance:</u>**
  - Architects, akin to skilled painters, rely on acute visual perception to envision and draft structures, while pilots, much like eagle-eyed navigators, depend on their sight to interpret myriad gauges and read landscapes from high above.

Through this accessible exploration, we see that our visual system is not just a passive window to the world but an active processor, vital for interpreting and interacting with our surroundings. Understanding this interplay of light and neurology not only enriches our comprehension of sight but also underscores the incredible complexity behind what many of us take for granted every time we open our eyes.

Our auditory system functions much like a high-fidelity sound system, capturing the symphony of life's soundtrack. When sound waves, akin to invisible ripples in the air, reach us, they are funneled by the ear's outer structure, just as speakers direct sound toward you. These waves then vibrate the eardrum – imagine this as the speaker's diaphragm trembling in response to a bass note. These vibrations are transferred through tiny bones, akin to the way a turntable's needle transmits the grooves' details to be amplified. The cochlea, resembling a coiled audio cable, translates these vibrations into electrical signals that the brain, our sound mixer, interprets as recognizable sounds, from the whisper of leaves to a friend's laughter. Understanding this process explains not just how we hear, but also how we can fine-tune our auditory attention and appreciate the nuances of communication and music. This understanding enhances our interaction with the world, making the simple act of listening a rich, multi-layered experience.

Here is the breakdown on the auditory system and its complex yet fascinating process of capturing and interpreting sound:

- **<u>Outer Ear:</u>**
    - **<u>Pinna:</u>** Like the dish of a satellite tuned to catch signals from space, the pinna gathers sound waves from our environment and directs them into the ear canal.
    - **<u>Ear Canal:</u>** Acting as the pathway or tunnel, the ear canal carries these captured sound waves with precision directly to the eardrum.

- **<u>Middle Ear:</u>**
    - **<u>Eardrum:</u>** The eardrum, akin to the tightly stretched skin of a drum, vibrates when struck by these sound waves, initiating a chain of amplification.
    - **<u>Ossicles:</u>** These are the three smallest bones in the body, functioning like a series of levers and hammers, that amplify and transmit the vibrations from the eardrum to the inner ear.

- **<u>Inner Ear:</u>**
    - **<u>Cochlea:</u>** Imagine the cochlea as a microphone's interior, where the

mechanical energy of sound vibrations is transformed into electrical signals by delicate hair cells floating in fluid.

- **Auditory Nerve:** This is the connection cable that carries the intricate electrical signals, as a sound engineer might route audio through wires, from the cochlea to the brain's sound editing suite.

- **Brain Processing:**
- **Temporal Lobe:** The temporal lobe serves as the brain's signal decoder, differentiating each sound wave frequency into familiar sounds, from a dog's bark to a symphony's crescendo.
- **Auditory Cortex:** This area acts like the soundboard at a music concert, fine-tuning the volume and pitch, and mixing the incoming audio, helping us recognize patterns like language or our favorite song.

By delving into each stage of this process, we understand that the simple act of hearing is, in fact, a highly technical concert performed by a series of biological structures. It is this very complexity that enables us to enjoy the subtleties of sound that enrich our lives, from engaging conversations to the stirrings of music. Understanding the auditory system this way not only educates but also brings a greater appreciation for the nuanced ways we experience the world through sound.

Imagine the kinesthetic system as a dancer engaged in an eloquent dance, where every movement communicates a message and each tactile sensation adds depth to that expression. This system is our body's way of feeling and moving through space. Just as a dancer is acutely aware of their body's position, our kinesthetic system helps us understand where each part of our body is and how it's moving, without needing to look. It lets us walk, even on a rocky path, without staring at our feet - much like an experienced dancer fluidly moves across the stage with perfect balance. Tactile sensations, the touch component of this system, inform us of texture and temperature, much like feeling the subtle differences between the smoothness of silk and the roughness of sandpaper or the warmth of a sunbeam and the chill of a breeze. It's a communication from our environment to our minds, that not only enables us to react but also to fully experience the world. This dance of movement and touch, so central to our lived experience, adds immeasurable richness to our daily lives, allowing us to physically connect with the people and places around us.

Here is the breakdown on the fascinating components of the kinesthetic system, which ensures our body's seamless movement and sensation of touch:

  - **<u>Proprioception:</u>**
    - **<u>Muscle Spindles:</u>**
    - Think of muscle spindles as tiny length meters nestled within your muscles, constantly measuring how stretched or contracted your muscles are and sending this information to the brain to help maintain posture and coordinate movement.
    - **<u>Joint Capsulators:</u>**
    - Joint capsules act as motion sensors embedded in your joints, providing the brain with real-time updates on the position of each joint, enabling the calculation of movements like the precise angle for catching a ball.
    - **<u>Vestibular System:</u>**
    - The vestibular system in your inner ear works similarly to an airplane's gyroscope, providing critical information about balance and spatial orientation so you can walk straight or spin around without losing your footing.

  - **<u>Touch:</u>**
    - **<u>Merkel Receptors:</u>**
    - Merkel receptors are akin to the fingertips of a sculptor, discerning the fine details and textures of surfaces, allowing you to appreciate the delicate weave of fabric or the roughness of tree bark.
    - **<u>Pacinian Corpuscles:</u>**
    - Pacinian corpuscles function like miniature vibration sensors, responding to deep pressure and rapid vibrations so you can feel the buzz of your phone in your pocket or the pounding bass at a concert.

By delving into each of these specialized sensors and mechanisms our body uses, we can appreciate how we physically interact with our world. It explains why we can perform complex tasks like playing a piano or recognize the gentle touch of a loved one. Through understanding proprioception and touch, we see how intrinsically connected we are to both our internal senses and the external world, highlighting the magic in the mundane act of simply experiencing physical sensation.

Think of the relationship between smell and taste as the culinary artistry involved in blending spices to create a flavorful dish. Just as individual spices have their own unique flavors, our sense of taste can detect distinct tastes—

sweet, salty, sour, bitter, and umami. Now, imagine these tastes as the base ingredients in your kitchen. Alone, each is simple, like the clarity of salt or the outright sweetness of sugar.

Enter the realm of aroma—like a complex spice blend, our sense of smell contributes depth and character to the perception of flavor. It's the saffron or cumin that transforms the base soup into an aromatic delight. Smell and taste work hand in hand, much like a chef expertly combining herbs and spices. As you eat, the food releases aromas that travel to your nose, enhancing and transforming the basic tastes detected by your tongue into the full experience of flavor.

This synergy turns the act of eating into a multisensory event; it's why a dish can evoke memories or emotions and why a stuffy nose can make even the spiciest curry seem bland. By understanding this partnership, much like recognizing the importance of seasoning in cooking, we begin to appreciate just how integral aroma is to our enjoyment of food and overall experience of the world around us.

Here is the breakdown on the intricate dance of biological mechanisms that intertwine smell and taste into the full-bodied experience of savoring a meal:

- **Taste Perception:**
  - **Taste Buds:**
  - Scattered across the tongue, taste buds are like specialized scouts, each capable of recognizing the five basic taste profiles: sweet, salty, sour, bitter, and umami. These are the front-line sentries that detect the initial features of your food.
  - **Taste Receptors:**
  - Within each taste bud are receptors that work like molecular keys fitting into locks, each designed to detect specific compounds, triggering signals that shoot up to the brain when they encounter their target taste molecule.

- **Smell Perception:**
  - **Olfactory Receptors:**
  - Nestled high in the nasal cavity, olfactory receptors are akin to an array of sophisticated sensors tuning in to various aromatic notes. They pick

up on a vast spectrum of volatile compounds, which we register as different scents.

- **Olfactory Bulb:**
    - Acting like a command center, the olfactory bulb processes these scent signals and then relays a detailed report to the brain, informing it of the aromatic complexities that are about to be experienced.

- **Integration in the Brain:**
- **Gustatory Cortex:**
    - The gustatory cortex is where taste information received is synthesized, rather like a master chef combining base ingredients with aromatic herbs to create a dish far greater than the sum of its parts.
- **Limbic System:**
    - The limbic system is where taste and aroma are interwoven with memory and emotion, much as certain spices can evoke memories of past meals or feelings of comfort.

By exploring these components, we learn just how layered our perception of flavor is. It's not merely about what touches the tongue but also what scents waft through the nose, contributing to a symphony of sensory information that creates the rich panorama of taste we cherish. This appreciation of how the body processes the elements of flavor can transform how we experience every bite, sip, and sniff, and bring us closer to understanding the depth of our sensory world.

In understanding how we perceive flavors, it's essential to recognize the joint effort of our taste and smell systems. Taste buds, located on the tongue, are dedicated to detecting the five well-known taste qualities: sweetness, sourness, saltiness, bitterness, and umami—a savory richness. These buds are adept at picking up these basic signals, which are then relayed to the brain for interpretation.

At the same time, inside the nasal cavity, olfactory receptors identify the aromas we inhale. These receptors handle a more complex spectrum of sensations, distinguishing between the thousands of volatile compounds that contribute to what we describe as smell. The olfactory bulb, which serves as an information hub, collects input from these receptors and channels it to the brain.

It's at the gustatory cortex where the information from both taste and smell is compiled, allowing for a complete perception of flavor. Additionally, the limbic system, closely interconnected with emotion and memory, means flavors can trigger recollections and feelings—enhancing the richness of our dining experiences. By paying attention to this relationship, one gains a better appreciation for the depth and complexity of flavor, not to mention a potentially heightened enjoyment of food.

Let's take a closer look at the intricate dance between taste and smell that creates our perception of flavor:

- **Taste Receptors:**
   - On our tongue, each taste bud houses receptors that function like little scouts, each tuned to specific taste molecules—sweet, salty, sour, bitter, or umami. When a molecule, such as sugar for sweetness, locks in with its corresponding receptor, it initiates a series of chemical events, resulting in an electric signal. This signal zips along a neural pathway to the brain, specifically to the gustatory cortex, where the brain interprets it as a taste sensation.

- **Olfaction Process:**
   - Imagine an aroma molecule as a scent messenger on a mission to find its specific receptor high up in our nasal cavity. Once they bind, a complex biological process converts this chemical interaction into an electrical signal. It's a bit like recognizing a familiar face in a crowd—once detected, the message is sent onwards to the olfactory bulb, our nasal command center.

- **Neural Pathways:**
   - The olfactory bulb acts as a mini-brain for smells, sorting these scent messages by their characteristics and priorities before sending them through the olfactory tracts to the brain. It meticulously organizes scent information which, when fused with the taste signals, enriches the perception of a full-bodied flavor.

- **Gustatory and Olfactory Integration:**
   - The gustatory cortex is like a gourmet chef who takes the base ingredients of taste and skillfully incorporates the complex aromas to create a delightful recipe of flavors. It's here where the collaboration of taste and smell signals occurs, allowing us to identify both basic and intricate flavors.

- <u>Influence of Emotion and Memory:</u>

- The limbic system, and especially the amygdala and hippocampus, work somewhat like a memory archive, cataloging the flavors associated with emotions and past experiences. Each savory bite or sniff can trigger vivid memories and emotional responses, contributing to the depth of our culinary experiences.

By dissecting these elements, it's evident that what might feel like simply enjoying a dish is actually a sophisticated symphony, played by our senses, that contributes to the multisensory delight of flavor. Understanding this interplay can transform the act of eating from a daily routine into a richer, more flavorful adventure.

Artists and designers, much like skilled chefs, skillfully blend a palette of sensory elements to craft experiences that can stir emotions or convey powerful messages. They combine colors, shapes, and textures in thought-provoking ways to evoke specific responses, similar to how the right mix of ingredients creates a memorable dish. Renowned public figures such as Steve Jobs intuitively understood the significance of sensory design in creating Apple's user-friendly interfaces, which evoke a sense of ease and efficiency. In the realm of visual art, creators like James Turrell manipulate light and space to immerse viewers in tranquil environments, inducing a sense of serenity and contemplation. Meanwhile, designers like Philippe Starck craft objects that please the eye while provoking thoughts about form and function, mirroring how a sculptor shapes materials to give form to emotions or ideas. These sensory manipulations are not mere happenstance; they are deliberate choices made to tap into our shared human experiences, revealing the potential of sensory design to resonate with our deepest sensibilities and enhance our interaction with the world.

Let's take a deeper look at the subtle yet powerful techniques artists and designers use to engage our senses:

- <u>Color Theory:</u>

- Much like a conductor selects the tones for an orchestra to stir emotions, color choices in design can set a mood or shift our perception. Warm colors might spark excitement or optimism, while cooler tones could bring about a sense of calm, illustrating the strategic use of color palettes to generate specific feelings in an audience.

- **Shape and Form:**

- The contours of forms in design can be as impactful as body language in conversation. Geometric shapes, with their clean lines and sharp angles, can convey order and precision, whereas organic shapes, with their curves and asymmetry, tend to evoke a sense of comfort and natural flow.

- **Texture and Materiality:**

- The selection of materials in design is akin to choosing the fabric for a garment, intending to engage the sense of touch. Designers today lean towards materials like wood and stone, not only for their tactile warmth but also to imbue objects with an aura of genuine quality and eco-consciousness.

- **Space and Light:**

- Imagine how the interplay of shadows and illumination in a room can transform an environment from a stage to an intimate nook. Through such manipulation of light and space, artists like James Turrell create atmospheres that can expand or encapsulate, guiding the viewer's emotional and spatial journey.

- **Ergonomics and Functionality:**

- The designs of Philippe Starck are testament to how form meets function with grace. His focus on ergonomics ensures that objects are not just visually striking but foster an intuitive and comfortable user experience, akin to how the design of a glove considers the natural curve of a hand.

Understanding these elements helps us see design not just as visual candy but as an experiential creation, echoing through our senses. It's a story told through hues, lines, textures, and the deft handling of space, proving that the detailed artistry behind our everyday objects and environments does more than catch the eye—it captivates the psyche.

This chapter has explored representational systems, which are the methods by which we interpret sensory information to understand our environment. These systems, encompassing visual, auditory, kinesthetic, olfactory, and gustatory senses, form the basis of our perception and play a critical role in how we interact with the world. By comprehending how these systems function, we can improve communication, enhance learning, and deepen our relationships both personally and professionally. Acknowledging the significance of representational systems in cognitive processes and behavioral patterns provides us with tools to fine-tune our sensory experiences and adapt effectively to our surroundings, enriching our lives in myriad ways.

SUBMODALITIES THE NUANCES OF EXPERIENCE

Welcome to "Submodalities: The Nuances of Experience," a chapter that opens the door to a deeper understanding of how the fine distinctions within our sensory experiences shape our thoughts, feelings, and actions. Submodalities are the subtle features of our sensory perceptions – the brightness or hue of a color, the volume or tone of a sound, the pressure or temperature of touch – that influence our emotional and mental states in powerful ways. By becoming aware of these nuanced qualities, we can learn to fine-tune our experiences and reactions in both our personal and professional lives. This chapter aims to guide you through the landscape of submodalities, revealing their crucial role not only in how we perceive the environment around us but also in how they serve as the undercurrent to our psychological experiences.

Submodalities are like the nuanced settings on your music player that help craft the perfect acoustic ambiance. Think about how adjusting the bass can deepen the pulse you feel in the air, or how increasing the treble brings out the shimmer in the high notes. Just as these auditory tweaks change the way a piece of music feels, submodalities adjust the texture of our sensory experiences. They're the brightness sliders, contrast knobs, and saturation levers for our mental imagery; the volume dials and equalizers for our internal dialogues; the thermostat and pressure settings for our physical sensations. Each small adjustment can transform a moment from forgettable to poignant, can render an experience more vivid, or can shift our emotional response to a memory. In essence, recognizing and altering submodalities allows us to be the sound engineers of our own sensory world, dialing in the mix that resonates best with our desired state of being.

In the realm of submodalities, specific attributes define and influence our sensory experiences. For visual experience, brightness is a key submodality— it determines how light or dark an image is, functioning much like a dimmer switch that can transform the mood of a photograph. In auditory experiences, pitch plays a pivotal role. It's the highness or lowness of a tone, akin to the notes on a piano keyboard, each producing a distinct sound that can be soothing or startling. As for kinesthetic experiences, which pertain to touch and movement, pressure is fundamental. It's the force applied—how a firm handshake conveys confidence or a gentle pat can comfort. These submodalities – brightness in vision, pitch in hearing, and pressure in touch – are the dials and gauges that calibrate our perception. Understanding how they function and interrelate offers the potential to transform our engagement with the world, sharpening our appreciation of both the subtleties and the intensities of our daily experiences.

To harness submodalities in a way that enriches your emotional well-being and communication, follow this step-by-step guide tailored for real-world practice:

Step 1: Identification
Begin by becoming aware of the sensory details in your experiences. This means actively noticing the fine points, like the precise hue of the green leaves in a park or the warm timbre in a friend's laugh. Becoming mindful of these details is the first step in recognizing the submodalities that shape your perception.

Step 2: Association
Next, connect certain submodalities to the feelings they invoke. Reflect on how a dimly lit room might make you feel relaxed, or a vibrant wall color energizes you. Understanding these associations is key to realizing how submodalities trigger different emotions.

Step 3: Adjustment
Now, experiment with changing submodalities in your mind to alter how you feel about a memory or situation. If recalling an event makes you anxious, try mentally adjusting the 'brightness' of that memory or 'softening' the sounds associated with it. By modifying these sensory details, you can shift the emotional weight they carry.

Step 4: Application
Take what you've practiced and apply it to your daily life. For instance, if you find yourself overwhelmed by a task, mentally 'mute' the background noise and focus on one 'color' or aspect to reduce the feeling of chaos. Applying these adjustments can help regulate your emotional responses.

Step 5: Habituation

Finally, make it a habit to monitor and adjust your submodalities regularly. The same way you might adjust a car's rearview mirror for the best view before driving, frequently check and refine the submodalities present in your day-to-day experiences to maintain emotional balance and enhance adaptability.

By following these steps, you progressively build the skill to manage your internal landscape, paving the way for improved emotional health and more effective communication.

Submodalities can be likened to the nuanced elements that compose the atmosphere of a room, each capable of shifting a person's mood. Imagine walking into a kitchen where the smell of freshly baked bread fills the air, the light is soft and golden, and a gentle tune plays in the background; the entire scene coaxes a feeling of warmth and homeliness. Now picture altering one element: replace the comforting melody with the blare of a traffic horn. Despite the pleasing aroma and light, your sense of calm is likely disrupted. This is submodality at work.

It's not only about what we perceive, but also how we perceive it. The volume, pitch, and tone of sounds; the intensity, hue, and saturation of colors; the pressure, texture, and temperature of an object—all contribute to our emotional reactions. Just as dimming the lights can create a romantic ambiance or amplifying the bass in a song can energize a crowd, subtly tweaking the submodalities of our experiences can change how we feel about them.

Through these everyday examples, we see the powerful role submodalities play in crafting our emotional responses. They are the dials and switches of our subconscious, adjusting the shades and sounds of our moment-to-moment life. By being conscious of and experimenting with these settings, we can influence our mood and perspective, making the world we perceive a more tailor-fit experience to our desires and needs.

Let's take a deeper look at the fascinating process of adjusting submodalities, those fine-tuned controls of our sensory experiences, to better steer our emotions and reactions:

- **<u>Step-by-Step Analysis of Submodalities:</u>**

Imagine your sensory perceptions as a personal control panel. Each control, from the brightness toggle akin to the dial on your sunglasses, making the world seem more brilliant or subdued, to the volume knob similar to your car stereo's, which can settle the cacophony of a busy street into a background hum, falls under your command. To amplify an element, such as the contrast in a visual scene, you might mentally enhance the darks and lights to make it more vivid, similar to adding extra seasoning to a dish for zing. To diminish an element, like the tempo of a song playing in your head, you could slow it down, envisioning a conductor guiding the orchestra to a more languid pace. It's about finding the right level for each sensory setting.

- <u>Emotional Calibration Techniques:</u>

Delving into the toolbox for emotional regulation, we find strategies to adjust the submodalities linked with strong emotions. For instance, to calm nerves before a speech, consciously adopt a slower speech pattern, emulating the unhurried flow of a leisurely stroll. Alternately, to soften the sharp edges of a stressful memory, you might mentally adjust its visual qualities, desaturating the colors or blurring the edges, as if viewing an old television with poor reception. Both tactics act to lower the emotional temperature, creating a buffer against overwhelm.

- <u>Practical Exercises for Daily Life:</u>

To bring this concept into daily practice, consider a routine exercise of realigning your submodalities. For moments when tension builds, practice breathing deeply while dimming the mental 'lights' of the issue, granting yourself a moment of twilight tranquility. Or, to amplify joy in a happy memory, concentrate on brightening the colors and sharpening the edges, much like enhancing a photograph on your phone to make it gallery-worthy. These exercises, done regularly, can train your emotional response system to be more responsive to your cues.

Through understanding how to adjust our perceptual submodalities, we can curate our emotional landscapes with precision and care, similar to creating the ideal ambiance within our homes. This mastery over our sensory inputs allows us to live more intentionally, react more constructively, and engage more authentically with the world around us.

To fine-tune your state of mind and bolster emotional well-being, here are some practical exercises to adjust your perceptual submodalities:

First, visualize a stressful situation. Now, play with the 'visual settings' of this image. Reduce its size, push it further away in your mind's eye, or drain it of color, turning it grayscale. These mental edits can dampen the associated emotional charge.

Next, let's target auditory submodalities. Think of an inner critical voice—perhaps it's loud and harsh. Mentally adjust this voice as if it were coming from a speaker. Turn down its volume, imagine it with a comical pitch, or change its distance, so it sounds as if it were far away. Altering how this voice sounds can change how you respond to it.

For kinesthetic feelings, such as anxiety, which might feel like pressure in your chest, imagine adjusting the sensation's intensity. Visualize a knob, like those on your stove, and mentally 'turn' it to regulate the feeling, dialing down from a simmer to a gentle warm.

These exercises act as rehearsals for managing emotions. Practicing them can make it easier to call on these techniques in real-life scenarios, providing more control over your experiences and reactions.

Here is the breakdown on the intricacies of practicing submodality adjustments, designed to navigate and regulate emotional states:

- **Visual Submodality Adjustments:**
  - **Size Adjustment:**
    - Identify a troubling image in your mind and consciously shrink it, as if using a remote to reduce its screen size, making it less intimidating.

  - **Distance Manipulation:**
    - Increase the mental space between yourself and the image. Imagine pushing it away from you, like a boat gently drifting off to sea, distancing the emotional impact.

  - **Color Alteration:**
    - Desaturate the colors of a negative memory gradually, like watching the vibrant colors of clothes fade after repeated washes, until it feels less vivid and emotionally charged.

- **<u>Auditory Submodality Adjustments:</u>**
- **<u>Volume Control:</u>**
- If a negative inner voice is too loud, mentally reach for an imaginary volume knob and turn it down as one would with a blaring radio, softening its influence on your emotions.

- **<u>Pitch Modification:</u>**
- Alter the pitch of the inner dialogue, shifting it to a more lighthearted tone, like playing with the voice settings on a recording app, to strip away the gravity of the words.

- **<u>Spatial Reorientation:</u>**
- Imagine the sound coming from a specific direction and gradually move it away from you, creating a sense of distance, as if the source of sound is walking away into the distance.

- **<u>Kinesthetic Submodality Adjustments:</u>**
- **<u>Pressure Adjustment:</u>**
- When feelings of anxiety surface, like a tight grip around your chest, envision a dial controlling this pressure and mentally turn it until the sensation loosens and eases.

- **<u>Temperature Tuning:</u>**
- For moments when emotions feel too hot, imagine adjusting a thermostat, bringing the temperature down to a cooler, more calming level, reducing emotional intensity.

These steps, familiar and grounded in everyday analogies, decode the process of modifying submodalities. By applying these strategies, you can work toward gaining mastery over your emotional reactions, effectively cultivating a more balanced mental state and improving your overall well-being and communication.

Consider the story of Michael Phelps, the Olympic swimmer whose mental preparation involved visualizing every aspect of his race in granular detail, down to the feel of the water on his skin. This is a prime example of fine-tuning visual and kinesthetic submodalities to achieve a level of focus and calm. Similarly, think about how a chef employs the submodality of taste, adjusting the intensity of flavors in a dish until the balance is just right—

modifying the 'salty' lever or the 'sour' dial to perfect a recipe.

In everyday life, submodalities are like the adjustments we do without thinking. When you lower the brightness on your phone screen at night, you're actually altering visual submodalities to prevent eye strain. Or when you change the volume of your music depending on whether you need calm or motivation—these are all adjustments of auditory submodalities tailored to your emotional state.

These examples emphasize how tweaking submodalities is not just a theoretical exercise, but a practical tool. They underline the relevance of understanding and adjusting these sensory elements, offering a pathway to enhance the way we live, work, and interact with others. Each adjustment, no matter how small, can be a powerful ally in managing our daily experiences and moods.

In the context of personal development and therapy, the practical application of submodalities has facilitated profound changes. Take, for example, a therapy session in which a client with a phobia is guided to alter the submodalities of their fear-inducing memory—perhaps dimming the imagery, muffling the sounds associated with it, or placing the memory at a 'safer' distance. By repeatedly practicing these adjustments, the client can experience a notable decrease in anxiety.

Let's consider another case where a professional speaker faced stage fright. By changing the internal representation of the audience—from an intimidating crowd to a group of supportive friends—and modulating the inner voice from a tremor of self-doubt to a confident tone, the speaker could step onto the stage with newfound poise.

These instances exemplify how subtle shifts in our sensory framework can result in significant emotional and behavioral changes. By dissecting these processes and understanding their mechanics, individuals harness the ability to remodel their internal experiences, thereby influencing how they feel and act in the external world. The potential of such techniques is not just theoretical but has been validated by real-life successes, affirming the power of submodalities as tools for transformation.

Let's take a deeper look at how submodalities can be harnessed for eliciting therapeutic change and personal development, turning seemingly abstract concepts into a practical toolkit:

- <u>Outline the Identification Process:</u>

- Start by exploring moments of discomfort or negativity, as if you were a detective analyzing clues at a crime scene. Delve into these memories or anticipations, and identify the 'flavors' of your experience, such as the vividness of the image or the decibel level of a sound. Make a mental note of these specifics: how bright or dim something is, how loud or soft, how near or far it feels.

- <u>Explain Adjustment Techniques:</u>

- Once you have pinpointed these submodalities, begin to bend and twist them like a photographer adjusts the focus on a camera. If a memory is too bright, mentally dial down its luminance, darkening the scene as you would adjust your living room lights for a movie night. If the internal critic is too loud, bring the volume to a whisper as if tuning a radio to the gentle hum of background music.

- <u>Detail Practice and Reinforcement:</u>

- For these changes to stick, incorporate them into your routine as you would a morning jog or evening meditation. Set aside time to mentally rehearse these adjustments, solidifying their effects. Practice not only dims the brightness of a harsh memory but layers it with a texture of neutrality. The reinforcement part is like learning a new language—regular use embeds the words into your vocabulary.

- <u>Explicate Outcome Measurement:</u>

- Keep a journal as a barometer for tracking shifts in your emotional climate. Monitor how your internal adjustments ripple out into the world around you. Do you react with less anger when the boss raises her voice? Do joyful moments feel brighter, more colorful? These observations are your metrics, gauges that tell you whether you are turning the dials in the right direction.

Understanding these steps and integrating them into your life is not unlike learning to drive—it's about gaining control over your vehicle of self-perception, navigating through the traffic of emotions and thoughts. As you become adept at steering your submodalities, you take charge of your psychological journey, leading to richer experiences and more intentional living.

In wrapping up 'Submodalities: The Nuances of Experience', we've journeyed through the critical role that these fine distinctions within our sensory perceptions play in shaping our emotions and behaviors. We've uncovered how adjusting the brightness, volume, or texture of our experiences can significantly affect our mental state. From the practical applications in therapy, helping individuals reshape troubling memories, to personal development methods that aid in overcoming fears like stage fright, submodalities have proven to be powerful levers of change. As we've seen, understanding and modifying these sensory dials enable us to fine-tune our internal experiences and, by extension, our reactions to the world—empowering us with the tools for enhanced emotional well-being and more effective communication. With these points in mind, the exploration of submodalities offers insightful strategies for constructing a more fulfilling and controlled emotional life.

LANGUAGE PATTERNS THE STRUCTURE OF PERSUASION

Persuasive language is a powerful tool that we wield daily, often without realizing its reach and impact. It is the art of using words not just to communicate but to influence and encourage others to see a different point of view or take action. This craft shapes our decisions and beliefs, filters through our interactions, and is the underpinning force in everything from advertising and political speeches to everyday discussions and debates. The effective use of persuasive language can lead to advancements in careers, societal changes, and personal successes. As we embark on this exploration of language patterns and the structures that make persuasion possible, we'll unlock the keys to not only understanding how influential language works but also to mastering its use in our own lives. Whether you are new to the subject or looking to refine your skills, this chapter will provide valuable insights into the strategic use of language for effective persuasion.

The bedrock of persuasive language lies in three core principles: ethos, logos, and pathos. Ethos refers to the credibility or ethical appeal of the speaker. It's about establishing trustworthiness and authority in a subject, much like a doctor's advice carries weight due to their expertise in medicine. Logos appeals to the audience's logical side by presenting clear, reasoned arguments. This is the data-driven aspect of persuasion, akin to a lawyer presenting evidence to support their case in court. Pathos, on the other hand, targets the listener's emotions. It's the storytelling part, evoking feelings of excitement, pity, or anger—emotions that can lead to action, in the same way charities might share heart-wrenching stories to inspire donations.

Understanding these elements is crucial for anyone looking to sharpen their persuasive abilities. They act as the pillars supporting the bridge of communication between the speaker and the listener. When used effectively and in balance, these principles can significantly strengthen the impact of a message.

Let's take a deeper look at the intricacies of ethos, logos, and pathos and understand how, like the strands of a rope, they intertwine to form a strong bond of persuasion.

- **Ethos** represents the integrity and credibility presented by the speaker. It comprises three main subcomponents:
  - **Expertise**: Like a pilot trusted to fly a plane, credentials in a particular field can establish one's authority to speak on a topic.
  - **Virtue**: The speaker's perceived character, akin to a trustworthy neighbor whose consistency and honesty have been proven over time.
  - **Charisma**: The subtle charm and confidence a speaker has, not unlike a captivating teacher whose presence commands the classroom.

Establishing ethos without existing authority is akin to a startup company seeking to establish its brand. A speaker might share personal stories that showcase their expertise, admit to not knowing everything but demonstrating a willingness to learn, or connect over shared values with the audience.

- **Logos** is about the logical structure of the argument itself, as foundational as the pillars supporting a building. It includes:
  - **Evidence**: Presenting hard data like a scientist showcasing research findings to support a hypothesis.
  - **Reasoning**: Carefully linking ideas together in a step-by-step argument that follows as clearly as a recipe in a cookbook.
  - **Avoidance of Fallacy**: Staying away from flawed logic, such as making sweeping generalizations or attacking the opposition, much like a chef carefully avoiding spoiled ingredients.

- **Pathos** reaches out to the audience's emotions, harnessing the same power as a gripping film that leaves viewers in tears.
  - **Storytelling**: Weaving a narrative that engages the audience emotionally, much like a grandparent recounting tales by the fireside.
  - **Language**: Selecting words that elicit emotional responses, as a poet chooses each word to stir the soul.
  - **Ethical Considerations**: Being mindful not to manipulate or exploit, just as a doctor takes care not to cause harm to a patient.

Mastering the use of ethos, logos, and pathos in discourse is akin to a chef adept in balancing flavors. Each element adds a unique essence, and when combined thoughtfully, they can engender respect, convince intellectually, and move emotionally, tailored to fit scenarios ranging from formal presentations to convincing a friend to join an adventure. Understanding these principles offers one the keys to unlock the art of persuasion in any walk of life.

Rhetorical structures like parallelism, antithesis, and tricolon are tools that can make language more impactful and memorable. Parallelism involves using the same pattern of words to show that two or more ideas have the same level of importance—similar to train cars on a track moving in harmony to the same destination. For example, a leader might say, "We must fight bravely, act wisely, and speak truthfully," using the structure to create a rhythm that underscores their points.

Antithesis is about contrasting ideas within a parallel structure, effectively setting two opposites against each other to highlight a stark difference— imagine a brightly lit room right next to a dark one, making the brightness stand out even more. A famous example from Charles Dickens starts with "It was the best of times, it was the worst of times," demonstrating this push and pull between ideas.

Tricolon is a series of three parallel elements or phrases; think of it as a three-course meal where each dish complements the others, providing a satisfying fullness. The intention is to create a series of escalating points, as in Julius Caesar's "I came; I saw; I conquered," leaving a lasting impression through brevity and power.

Each of these structures weaves complexity into speech and writing in a way that makes the content not just understood but felt. They are the threads that can tie together a narrative, paint a picture of contrast, or deliver a powerful punch. Mastery of these rhetorical tools can enhance communication in both the written and spoken word, imbuing the speaker's messages with elegance, force, and persuasion.

To incorporate the rhetorical structures of parallelism, antithesis, and tricolon into your writing or speaking, follow this practical guide:

- **Parallelism**:
1. Identify the core message you want to convey. This will be the foundation for your parallel structure.
2. Choose a pattern of words, whether it's a starting word, a grammatical structure, or a thematic concept to repeat.
3. Construct a series of phrases or sentences that follow your chosen pattern, ensuring each carries a similar weight in the progression of your

argument.

4. Use this technique to enforce rhythm and make your point resonate, much like a drumbeat in a song.

For example, if advocating for healthy habits, you might say, "Eating wisely, exercising regularly, and sleeping sufficiently are the pillars of good health."

- **Antithesis**:

1. Start by determining two opposing ideas you want to juxtapose to create a compelling argument.

2. Craft a statement that clearly presents these contrasting ideas in a balanced way.

3. Use parallel structures for both halves of the statement to enhance the impact of the contrast.

4. Utilize antithesis to emphasize a choice or a difference, compelling the audience to consider both sides.

An instance of antithesis might be: "To err is human; to forgive, divine," showcasing the contrast between human fallibility and the lofty ideal of forgiveness.

- **Tricolon**:

1. Pinpoint the climax of your argument where a reinforcing series of statements will be most effective.

2. Develop three succinct, parallel phrases that build upon each other in intensity or significance.

3. Ensure brevity and rhythm; like the beats of a heart, the tricolon should pulse with growing force.

4. Apply this technique to hammer home a point with escalating power, leaving a lingering impact.

For instance, a politician might use a tricolon for emphasis: "This legislation will bring support, stability, and success to our schools."

By methodically applying these tools, you can craft language that's not only heard but felt. The calculated use of parallelism creates harmony, antithesis sharpens differences, and tricolon amplifies your message's impact. Together, they form a powerful ensemble in the art of persuasion.

Think of the expert persuader's techniques much like a set of tools in a craftsman's kit. Each tool has a specific purpose, designed with precision to shape the material at hand into a desired outcome. The hammer, strong and decisive, like bold statements and authoritative declarations, drives points home. A chisel, equivalent to storytelling, carves out narratives that grip listeners, shaping their thoughts subtly and intricately. Sandpaper, mirroring the art of rhetorical questioning, smooths away at the audience's resistance, gradually refining rough edges of skepticism.

Then there's the measuring tape; experts use this tool to tailor their message to their audience's values and beliefs, ensuring a perfect fit. The level is used to find balance in arguments, much like the careful arrangement of factual and emotional appeals. And let's not forget the saw, symbolic of humor and wit, which can cut through tension and open up an audience to more serious discourse that follows.

In the hands of a skilled user, these instruments of persuasion create more than just a finished product—they craft experiences, forge connections, and align audiences with the speaker's vision. Just as a well-made piece of furniture stands out in a room, a well-constructed argument resonates in the minds of those who hear it. Each technique, when used with care and attention, contributes to the incredible potential of language to inspire, motivate, and influence.

Here is the breakdown on how to use persuasive techniques paralleled with a craftsman's toolkit, providing a hands-on approach to mastering the art of persuasion:

- **<u>The Hammer (Bold Statements and Authoritative Declarations):</u>**
  - **<u>Crafting Impactful Statements:</u>**
    - Begin with a solid fact or irrefutable baseline to establish ground authority.
    - Employ declarative sentences that are short and to the point, akin to the firm strike of a hammer.
  - **<u>Formulating Authoritative Tone:</u>**
    - Use active voice to convey confidence, much like a craftsman assertively wielding a tool.

- Incorporate strong, specific verbs that drive action and command attention.

- **<u>The Chisel (Storytelling):</u>**
  - **<u>Elements of a Compelling Narrative:</u>**
  - Establish the setting – Create a relatable backdrop for your story as a sculptor chooses the right wood or stone for their art.
  - Introduce conflict – Present challenges that resonate with common struggles, engaging the audience with familiarity.
  - Lead to resolution – Guide the audience through the narrative arc to a satisfying conclusion, much like the chiseling away to reveal the sculpture's form.
  - **<u>Integrating Narrative in Arguments:</u>**
  - Weave personal anecdotes that parallel the logical points of your argument, ensuring a blend of logos and pathos.
  - Highlight real-life examples that align with your persuasive goals – stories that serve as a microcosm of the larger message you are conveying.

- **<u>The Sandpaper (Rhetorical Questioning):</u>**
  - **<u>Constructing Probing Questions:</u>**
  - Frame questions that naturally lead the audience to contemplate and question their current stance, as sandpaper smooths wood grain.
  - Ask questions that evoke curiosity but don't demand direct answers, allowing the audience to ponder internally.
  - **<u>Following Up With Evidence:</u>**
  - Present data and facts immediately after rhetorical questions to fill the spaces opened by inquiry.
  - Offer logical explanations that address potential biases or doubts raised by the initial questions, progressively leading to a more polished perspective.

Utilizing these tools, much like a craftsman bringing together diverse elements to create a cohesive and beautiful piece, allows a speaker or writer to craft messages that not only inform but also resonate on a deeper emotional level. As you familiarize yourself with these persuasive 'tools,' practice becomes key—shaping your language into an art form that leaves a lasting impression on your audience.

To grasp the effectiveness of language patterns, let's look at public figures renowned for their rhetoric. Consider Barack Obama, whose cadence and pauses are akin to a conductor's control over an orchestra, commanding attention and establishing a rhythm that resonates with his audience. His speeches often begin with a calm, steady pace, drawing listeners in, before escalating to powerful crescendos, driving his points home.

Steve Jobs, too, mastered the art of the product reveal, using simple, emphatic expressions reminiscent of an artist unveiling a long-awaited masterpiece. Jobs' presentations were stripped of any complex jargon, and instead, he used relatable anecdotes and awe-inspiring visuals to let the product's innovation speak for itself.

Even historical figures like Winston Churchill demonstrated unparalleled command over persuasion through language patterns. Churchill's speeches, brimming with parallel structures and poignant analogies, were like verbal blitzes that fortified the resolve of a nation under siege.

These case studies exemplify how language patterns aren't just mechanics of speech but are the brushstrokes of spoken artistry that can paint ideas into the public consciousness. Through their words, these figures didn't just communicate; they captivated, inspired, and moved nations. Understanding and adopting the essence of their language patterns can elevate one's communication from mere talk to impactful discourse.

Let's take a deeper look at the fine details of rhetoric used by Barack Obama, Steve Jobs, and Winston Churchill, breaking down their language patterns:

- **<u>Barack Obama</u>:** Obama's speeches are often structured with a methodical build-up. His sentences start short and simple, setting a clear, digestible foundation – akin to the first few steps of a staircase. Gradually, he introduces more complex sentences, layering them with subordinate clauses that add depth, much like adding floors to a skyscraper. The tempo of his speech initially mirrors a steady walk, then transitions into a run as he builds towards a crescendo. Pauses are strategically placed, creating suspense akin to a brief silence between the movements of a symphony, before charging forward to his salient point.

- **<u>Steve Jobs</u>:** Jobs was a maestro at unveiling products. He used descriptive language to create vivid images, almost as if he was painting the features in the listener's mind. His knack for simplifying complex technical terms into everyday language can be likened to translating a foreign language into layman's terms, making the information accessible to all. The narrative arc of his presentations carried the suspense and excitement of a novel, leading to the climax of revealing the product, much like the final, page-turning chapter of a thriller.

- **<u>Winston Churchill</u>:** Churchill's speeches employed parallel structures to emphasize the gravity and urgency of the situation. A distinct pattern, such as "We shall fight on the beaches, we shall fight on the landing grounds," reinforces the point through repetition, echoing the relentlessness of waves crashing onto shore. His analogies were crafted to resonate with his countrymen's experiences, using imagery from their everyday lives to illustrate broader war efforts, thereby lending both familiarity and dignity to their struggles.

Understanding the nuances of these skilled communicators allows us to see the mechanics of what makes their language so impactful. It's like understanding a recipe – once you know the ingredients and the steps, you can replicate and perhaps even improve on the original. By dissecting these methods, we gain insights into crafting messages that not only inform but also inspire and drive action.

In media and marketing, persuasive language is a key player, functioning much like the engine in a car, propelling messages forward and driving consumer actions. Take the classic 'Just Do It' slogan from Nike, which employs brevity and the imperative form to instill a sense of immediate action. It's a call to break inertia, much like a coach's motivational shout to an athlete.

Likewise, in television commercials, advertisers often create a storyline around a product, painting it as a hero that solves a consumer's problem. A car isn't just a vehicle but a passport to adventure; a laundry detergent not merely a cleaning agent, but a guardian of family health. These narratives use simplified language and poignant imagery to forge an emotional connection between the product and the audience – a connection designed to linger long after the advertisement has ended.

Furthermore, consider Apple's marketing, which often highlights the sophisticated design and innovation of its products with sleek visuals and a minimalist approach. This mirrors the concept of 'less is more', allowing the product's elegance to stand out without clutter – similar to an artist showcasing a single masterpiece in an empty gallery.

In these instances, the persuasive language of media and marketing does more than inform about a product; it infuses the product with values and emotions that resonate with the audience's aspirations. By drawing clear links between these marketing techniques and the discussed concepts of persuasive language, we can observe a harmonious blend of ethos, pathos, and logos in action, all geared towards the ultimate goal of persuasion.

When crafting a persuasive marketing campaign, the interplay of ethos, pathos, and logos is key to resonating with the audience. Let's guide you through this neatly.

Starting with a compelling slogan, such as Nike's iconic 'Just Do It,' consider the words carefully. The choice should be short, memorable, and powerful. Using the imperative form serves as a command which, coupled with Nike's historical association with sports excellence, acts as a rallying cry that taps into the cultural ethos of determination and achievement. The slogan's ability to induce action is rooted in its psychological impact—think of it as the last push someone needs to start their fitness journey.

Moving to emotionally engaging commercials, the story often centralizes around the product solving a pressing issue or improving the consumer's life. It starts by identifying with the audience's problem or desire. Visual and auditory elements are curated to evoke the right emotions—like the warmth of a family meal or the adrenaline rush of an adventure—all timed perfectly with the message to captivate the audience. This method forges a pathos-driven bond, positioning the product as not just a mere object but a key to a better experience.

For a minimalist approach, such as that exemplified by Apple, less is indeed more. The focus is on the product's design and features, presented against a clean and clutter-free background. Apple utilizes a logos-driven strategy, appealing to the logic of needing a user-friendly yet technologically advanced product. The simplicity in design and messaging conveys sophistication, suggesting that the user will be part of an exclusive group by choosing their brand, thereby appealing to both ethos and pathos.

This methodology, from inception to execution, demonstrates that understanding and leveraging the principles of persuasion can significantly elevate a marketing campaign's efficacy. Each element contributes to creating a narrative that not only informs but also inspires and propels the audience towards action.

To effectively apply persuasive language in daily life, practice is key, much like rehearsing a play until the lines are delivered with natural flair. Start with an exercise to hone your ethos: spend a day noting down moments where you naturally establish credibility, whether it's sharing expertise at work or giving advice to a friend. Notice the language you use that conveys your experience and trustworthiness. For logos, try breaking down a complex topic you are familiar with into simple explanations, as if teaching it to a child or someone entirely unfamiliar with the subject. This will help you refine clear, logical communication.

Pathos can be practiced by sharing a personal story and observing the emotional reactions from your audience. Learn which parts of your story evoke responses and analyze why. Finally, as a comprehensive exercise, write a short persuasive speech on a topic you're passionate about, deliberately weaving ethos, logos, and pathos into your narrative. Present this to friends or family and invite their feedback on which parts they found most compelling.

Remember, persuasive language is a powerful tool, like a chef's knife that must be handled with care and skill, sharpened through consistent use. These exercises will not only bolster your persuasive abilities but also deepen your understanding of the impact your words can have on others.

Here is the breakdown of activities to fine-tune your use of ethos, logos, and pathos in everyday communication, presented in a way that's as straightforward as consulting a how-to manual or recipe book:

- **Ethos:**
  - **Documenting Credentials:**
    - Keep a running list of your formal education, training, and major

achievements to naturally reference during discussions.

- Think of this list as a tool belt, each item a tool that's perfect for a specific job.

- **Application in Conversation:**

- Envision real-life situations, like job interviews or debates, where showcasing your expertise is key.

- Prepare concise statements that incorporate your credentials without disrupting the natural flow of discussion, as seamlessly as a chef adds spices to a dish.

- **Logos:**
- **Outlining Complex Ideas:**

- Select a topic you're well-versed in, like sustainable living or technology advancements.

- Piece apart this topic into simple components, as if dissecting a machine to understand how it works.

- **Crafting a Lesson Plan:**

- Develop a brief guide with key takeaways that anyone, from a child to an adult, can grasp.

- Structure this guide like stepping stones across a stream, making the path clear and the crossing easy.

- **Pathos:**
- **Identifying Emotional Stories:**

- Reflect on moments of your life that have made a strong impression on friends or family.

- Find the core emotion of these stories, like finding the heart of a matter.

- **Sharing for Impact:**

- Plan out the storytelling, focusing on language that evokes the desired emotion, much like painting a picture with the goal of evoking a specific feeling.

- Look for the right times to share these stories, when they can deeply resonate with listeners, just as a song might move a person when the mood is just right.

Adopting these techniques is akin to learning to play new chords on a guitar, where practice and timing can turn simple strums into harmonious music. With regular practice and application, you can wield persuasive language with the finesse of an artisan, crafting messages that not only inform but also resonate and inspire.

In this chapter, we've explored the profound influence of persuasive language and its three pillars: ethos, logos, and pathos. By understanding ethos, we've learned the value of establishing credibility and the weight that character and expertise lend to our words. Logos has shown us the power of a well-structured argument and the importance of supporting it with clear logic and evidence. Pathos has opened our eyes to the emotional connections that can envelop and guide an audience toward a desired response. Together, these elements of persuasive language act as a toolkit for speakers and writers, spurring others to see, feel, and act differently. This knowledge equips us with the ability to not just communicate but to affect change, urging us to use language responsibly and with awareness of its potential impact on thoughts, beliefs, and behaviors.

ANCHORING TRIGGERING RESOURCEFUL STATES

Anchoring within the practice of Neuro-Linguistic Programming, or NLP, offers individuals a practical method to deliberately access their most resourceful emotional states when desired. It operates on the principle of association—the psychological link between a particular stimulus and an emotional response. By creating anchors, or triggers, you can elicit positive feelings and attitudes, such as calm or confidence, on cue. This technique can significantly enhance personal effectiveness in challenging situations, such as public speaking, competition, or high-stress environments. It equips you with the emotional agility to manage your internal state, ensuring that you can perform at your best when it matters most. This introductory chapter unfolds the essence of anchoring and its application, aiming to empower you with the skills to leverage your emotional responses for a more successful and centered life.

Anchoring in NLP is akin to creating a fast-track path to specific emotions. You establish a physical 'trigger', such as a gentle tap on your wrist, coinciding with a peak emotional state. Later, using that same gesture can help you instantly revisit the targeted feeling. This process cuts through the noise of our busy minds, offering a direct line to the emotional responses we want to harness. It's as straightforward as bookmarking a page in a book for easy return—a simple action with powerful results. With proper setup and practice, this strategy allows for quick access to a state of mind that might otherwise require more time and effort to achieve. It's an especially useful tool when facing situations that demand confidence, focus, or calm. By utilising this technique, we can shift into a preferred emotional gear almost instantly, providing an edge in both personal and professional contexts.

Step 1: Begin by identifying an emotional state that you would like to access on command, such as a feeling of confidence, calmness, or happiness. Close your eyes and bring up a memory where you felt this emotion strongly. Immerse yourself in this recollection, noticing the details: what you saw, heard, and felt.

Step 2: Next, select a physical trigger that will be your anchor. This could be a touch of your thumb and forefinger together, pressing your palm, or any discreet action that you can perform anytime. Ensure it's something simple that doesn't attract attention and that you don't do it involuntarily.

Step 3: At the moment when the emotional state is at its peak during your recollection, initiate the physical trigger. Hold the trigger for a few seconds while you continue to experience the emotion fully.

Step 4: Reinforce the anchor through repetition. Over the next days, revisit this emotional state and trigger the physical action again. Do this at least five times to strengthen the association. Timing is crucial - the trigger must occur at the peak of the emotional experience to be effective.

Step 5: Put the anchor to use in real-life situations when you need the emotional state the most. For instance, if you anchored confidence, use the trigger before walking into a job interview. If it's calm you've anchored, apply it when you start to feel stressed, such as before giving a presentation or in a moment of conflict.

By following these steps, the anchor becomes a reliable way to shift your internal state, giving you greater control over your reactions and empowering you to be at your best when it's most crucial.

To master the art of anchoring in NLP, start by pinpointing a positive emotional state you'd like to be able to call upon at will—perhaps it's the zest from a successful project or the serenity from a weekend at the beach. Sit quietly and delve into these memories, stirring up as vivid a sensation as possible.

Next, choose a physical stimulus that will act as your anchor; this could be as subtle as a knuckle rub or as personal as a necklace touch. It should be discrete, something you can steer clear of doing absently, to maintain its significance.

Now, as you bask in the warmth of your chosen emotion, introduce your anchor. Press your fingers together or touch the necklace, creating a concrete connection between the physical act and your emotional state.

Repeat this conditioning process several times over days or weeks. The more consistently you do this, the stronger the linkage becomes. Think of it as forging a new pathway in your brain, one that—once solidified—allows you to trigger this emotional state on demand.

Remember, success with anchoring comes from the quality of the emotional state and the consistency of your practice. Use this guide to hone an inner emotional toolkit, empowering yourself to take on life's various moments with your chosen state of mind.

Let's take a deeper look at the intricacies of anchoring, starting by choosing a suitable emotional state. Imagine you're shopping for ingredients to create a gourmet dish—the chosen emotion must be intense, pure, and memorable, like selecting the freshest and most flavorful produce. This emotional state should be one you can remember vividly and stir up at will, with rich details akin to a vibrant taste lingering on your palate.

When deepening the emotional state, think of turning up the color on a high-definition screen. Immerse yourself in the memory fully, with every sense heightened. If your memory is of a day at the beach, recall the warm sun on your skin, the rhythmic lull of waves, the salty breeze—the more sensorial details, the more effective the anchoring will be.

Pinpointing the exact moment of peak emotional intensity is like capturing the spark of a match igniting. It's sharp, sudden, and unmistakable. Only when you're basking in the full glow of this emotion should you introduce your chosen physical trigger. It's a delicate dance of timing that requires self-awareness and practice.

For the personalization of the physical trigger, think of it as designing your own signature sign-off on a letter. It may be as individual as the way you smile or as unique as a discreet movement you make. This physical trigger should meld seamlessly into your life's patterns, befitting your personal style and disposable at any moment like your favorite pair of sunglasses.

As for reinforcing the anchor, consistent practice is key. Much like watering a plant to see it flourish, trigger your anchor several times over the following days and weeks to solidify the association. Integrate this into your routine when you naturally feel the emotion or during dedicated quiet moments, ensuring the anchor grows robust like a deeply rooted tree.

Employing anchoring with such refined attention to detail will ensure the technique becomes a reliable part of your emotional toolkit. And just as you'd savor a well-crafted meal, you'll appreciate the nuances that make this NLP method not just effective but a critical asset for navigating life's ebb and flow.

In the realm of public speaking, consider a speaker who squeezes a stress ball backstage just before delivering a riveting speech. This action isn't solely to release tension; it's an anchor, previously set to evoke a flood of confidence. Similarly, an athlete may kiss a medallion before a race, summoning the same surge of adrenaline and focus that powered through rigorous training sessions. It's these small, intentional actions that call forth the precise emotions needed to excel.

Anchoring can also be a tranquil harbor in the storm of daily stress. Someone might employ a deep breathing technique paired with a mantra, anchoring relaxation to this routine. When the bustle of life picks up, a few focused breaths can whisk them back to tranquility, much like a comforting rhythm can soothe an agitated mind.

These examples show anchoring as a stealthy ally in our pursuit of success and serenity. It's not just about handling the moment; it's about steering our emotional state with intention, using established personal cues to gear up for the presentation, competition, or simply to navigate the day's anxieties with a steadier hand.

Here is the breakdown on establishing enduring anchors in the formative phase of anchoring:

- **<u>Selecting an Anchor:</u>**
  - Considerations:
    - Choose a trigger subtle enough to go unnoticed by others but distinctive to you, like the motion of adjusting a watch.
    - It should be easily replicated, ensuring you can do it anywhere without drawing attention, reminiscent of silently setting a reminder on your phone.

- Personalization:
- Find a trigger that has personal significance or is a natural part of your behavior, such as a specific way you fold your hands or a particular pattern of finger tapping.

- **<u>Conditioning Process:</u>**
- Creating the Emotional State:
- Revisit a potent, joyful memory or imagine an achievement with rich detail, including surrounding sounds, colors, and feelings, mirroring the intensity of watching a movie in a theater.

- Association:
- Introduce your trigger at the peak of the emotional experience multiple times, akin to saving a favorite song in a playlist to hit play when needed.
- Use varied levels of emotional intensity to ensure the association is strong across different situations, much like adjusting the brightness for visibility in diverse lighting.

- Testing Effectiveness:
- Try activating the anchor after a few days to see if it elicits the emotion, similar to checking if a saved contact in your phone rings the right person.

- **<u>Reinforcement Strategies:</u>**
- Frequency and Context:
- Regularly reinforce the anchor in both calm and mildly stressful situations to 'proof' it against different emotional climates, much like seasoning food to taste right in both cold and warm conditions.

- Integration into Routine:
- Incorporate your anchor into daily events, like using it each morning to start the day positively, or during routine breaks, just as you might stretch your legs on a long flight for comfort and to maintain flexibility.

These careful steps will construct a robust framework for your NLP anchoring practice. By infusing these techniques into day-to-day life, you create a reliable resource to swiftly realign your emotional state, preparing you to face an array of challenges with resilience and grace, much as a well-prepared traveler navigates new terrains with ease and confidence.

Consistently using an anchor in NLP, much like practicing a musical instrument, strengthens your proficiency and access to the emotional state it triggers. Every time you activate the anchor—the physical gesture or touch that you have associated with a positive emotion—you reinforce the neurological pathways responsible for calling up this state. It's as if each repeated activation polishes a pathway in your mind until it's so well-trodden that the mere hint of the stimulus begins to bring the emotion to the forefront. This repetition builds a strong, almost automatic response, streamlining the process of entering the desired state. Before long, the anchor becomes an efficient mental shortcut, allowing you to tap into empowering emotions with the simplicity and speed of flicking on a light switch. Over time, with regular use in various contexts, this practice helps you maintain an emotional equilibrium, making the beneficial state not just a conscious choice but a ready-to-use tool in your emotional arsenal.

Let's take a deeper look at the neurological craftwork behind reinforcing anchors in NLP. Just as a pathway in a forest becomes clearer and easier to travel with frequent use, so too does the neural path between a physical trigger and an emotional state become more established with repetition. Every time you activate your anchor, it's like sending a signal along this path. The more signals sent, the stronger and more pronounced the pathway becomes, facilitating quicker and more intense access to the desired state.

Consistency in this practice is vital. It's akin to watering a plant; regular care is essential to its growth. For an anchor to take root effectively, it should be activated consistently, with the frequency calibrated just like the strings of a guitar—neither too tight nor too slack. Integrating the use of anchors into daily routines, or during times of emotional relevance, can help fortify the association, much like infusing a daily cup of tea with a favorite flavor.

To track the progress and potency of an anchor, one might keep a journal, documenting each activation of the trigger and the ensuing emotional experience. Over time, you'll notice patterns, with the emotional response becoming more swift and potent with each use. Should the anchor's effect start to wane, it may signal the need to adjust your practice—perhaps by choosing a stronger initial emotional memory, like selecting a more vibrant color to refresh a fading painting.

Understanding these dimensions enriches your anchoring technique, turning it from a mere concept to a dynamic, personal tool. With this knowledge, you're not just pulling a lever to initiate an emotional state; you're tuning an instrument with the potential to harmonize your inner world, playing the chords that resonate with your aspirations and well-being.

When building anchors in NLP, a common hurdle is creating one that seems to lack strength or consistency – basically, an underpowered anchor. It's similar to learning to ride a bike and finding that you can't quite maintain balance yet. The anchor, much like the bike, isn't serving its purpose if it can't support you when you need it.

The solution often lies in recalibration. For the cyclist, it might mean adjusting the seat height. In anchoring, it may involve revisiting the emotional state you've chosen to ensure it's intense and vivid enough. If the connection feels weak, returning to the memory of that emotion and re-engaging with it more deeply can help. You can also try a different physical trigger, just as you might try a bicycle with a different frame to find the right fit.

Another adjustment is to practice activating your anchor in a quiet, focused setting, free from distractions, reinforcing the link without interference. Just as a novice cyclist starts on a smooth, straight path to build skill, so should you create an environment conducive to strengthening your anchor. With time, patience, and these targeted strategies, your anchors will become robust tools, ready to steady and propel you forward, just as getting the hang of biking eventually leads to a smooth, enjoyable ride.

Here is the breakdown on enhancing the effectiveness of underpowered anchors in a way that's as easy to follow as a favorite recipe:

- **<u>Assessing the Anchor's Strength:</u>**
  - Indicators of Strength:
    - A strong anchor is like a reliable old friend; it shows up and delivers consistently. When activated, it promptly evokes a vivid emotional state.
    - An underpowered anchor is like a weak handshake; it fails to make an impression or bring the emotional state into sharp relief.

  - Methods for Self-Assessment:

- Self-assessment could mirror asking, "How did that feel?" after trying something new. Reflect on whether the anchor elicits the emotion with immediacy and intensity.

- For feedback, like checking with a friend if your outfit works for an occasion, you can ask trusted peers to observe your demeanor when you use the anchor, checking for visible shifts in your emotional state.

- **Intensifying the Emotional State:**
- Deepening Techniques:
- Enhancing the emotion is like turning up the volume on your favorite song. Use guided imagery exercises, imagine the scenario with rich details, or employ sensory recall: picture the scene, hear the sounds, and invoke related scents or textures.

- **Varying the Physical Trigger:**
- Selection of Triggers:
- Choose a trigger like you would pick out accessories for an outfit—it should complement you and not feel out of place. These can range from tapping a finger to reciting a word internally.

- The criteria for effectiveness is similar to finding the perfect temperature for your shower. It must be just right for you: comfortable to perform and easy to remember.

- **Creating a Conducive Environment:**
- Setting Enhancement:
- Create a practice space like you'd set a stage for a play. It should be free from distractions, quiet, and pleasant, setting the mood for you to focus solely on the anchoring process.

- **Reinforcement Schedule:**
- Recommended Schedule:
- Establishing a routine can be like setting up a fitness regimen. Aim for a schedule that suits your daily life, regularly performing the anchor, and maintain this pattern for at least a few weeks to let the neural connection take root and flourish.

By understanding these components, readers can integrate anchoring into their lives with the finesse of a skilled chef creating a culinary masterpiece.

It's not just the ingredients that matter, but the care in preparation—creating anchors that not only work but work wonders for you.

Integrating anchoring into your daily routine can be as seamless as forming any other habitual activity, such as your morning jog or nightly meditation session. Imagine tying your running shoes before a run or lighting a scented candle before meditation – these actions signal to your body that it's time for a certain activity. Similarly, use your anchoring gesture – like touching a pendant or pressing your fingers together – right before beginning tasks that resonate with the emotional state you want to invoke.

For instance, activate your confidence anchor before starting your workday, just like stretching before exercise, to set a tone of self-assurance. Or engage the anchor for calmness as you sit down to pay bills, akin to clearing your mind before meditating. Over time, just as the body learns to release endorphins when you lace up your running shoes, your mind will begin to automatically summon the desired emotion when you perform your anchor, weaving it into the fabric of your life as naturally as your evening wind-down routine. This practice turns anchoring into a powerful, subconscious undercurrent that supports your well-being throughout the day.

Here is the breakdown on interweaving the principles of habit formation with the strengthening of NLP anchors:

- **<u>Habit Formation Basics:</u>**
  - Stages of Habit Formation:
    - Cue: The triggering event or sensation, like the smell of coffee that prompts your morning routine.
    - Routine: The action you take in response to the cue, akin to brewing a pot and sipping your first cup.
    - Reward: The positive feeling or outcome reinforcing the habit, closely resembling the satisfaction of a warm caffeine boost.
    - Anchoring Parallel: Associate your anchor with a cue (a specific time or emotional state), execute the routine (engaging your anchor), and enjoy the reward (the empowered emotional state).

  - Role of Consistency:
    - Just as daily workouts lead to improved fitness, regularly activating your anchor reinforces its effectiveness and your ability to enter the desired

emotional state.

- **<u>Neurological Correlation:</u>**
  - Brain's Role in Habits:
  - Neural pathways, like well-worn footpaths, develop through constant use. Each activation of your anchor treads this path, making the route more familiar and accessible.

- **<u>Tailoring Anchors to Habits:</u>**
  - Selecting Routine Activities:
  - Embed anchors in everyday actions. For focus, use an anchor while your computer boots up; for motivation, activate it as you write your to-do list.

  - Environmental Cues:
  - Set physical reminders in your environment to use your anchor, much like gym clothes laid out the night before nudging you towards a morning workout.

- **<u>Monitoring and Adjusting:</u>**
  - Tracking Effectiveness:
  - Keep a journal of your emotional responses after using your anchor, similar to a fitness tracker logging your exercise progress.
  - Observe yourself: If the anchor is not eliciting the desired state, tweak your trigger or the intensity of the emotional memory linked to it.

By layering these details, like fine stitching on a bespoke garment, your anchors become tailor-made supports, enhancing your daily life with a surge of self-crafted inspiration.

Auditory and visual anchors in NLP are like the subtle cues an actor uses to get into character, or the background music that sets the mood in a film—they subtly but significantly influence our emotional states. Auditory anchors could be a specific song, a certain tone of voice, or a personal mantra that, when heard, transports you to a desired emotional land. Think of the chime that reminds you it's time to start a meditation session, indicating a shift from the hustle of life to a moment of tranquility.

Visual anchors involve using a symbolic image, a color, or even a particular sight, such as the view from a window, to evoke an emotion or state of mind. It might be as simple as a photograph that reminds you to feel gratitude or a sticky note in a bright color placed on your desk that nudges you to stay focused on your goals.

Layering these types of anchors means involving multiple senses to enrich the cue for your emotional state. It's like enjoying a meal where the presentation, aroma, and flavors all combine to create a more intense experience. By integrating an auditory cue like a calming piece of music with a visual one like a serene landscape, you can create a more complex and powerful anchor that can more effectively summon the desired emotional state.

Let's take a deeper look at the art of choosing and intertwining auditory and visual anchors to bolster your NLP toolkit:

- **Selection Criteria for Auditory Anchors:**
  - Memorable Factors:
    - Just as a catchy jingle sticks with you throughout the day, an auditory anchor should be distinct and memorable. Consider how certain rhythms or melodies effortlessly recall past experiences and emotions.
    - Evaluate the emotional undertones of various sounds; for instance, the calming quality of raindrops or the energizing effect of a drumbeat, linking them to personal experiences that evoke strong emotional responses.

  - Mantras and Tones:
    - Crafting a personal mantra is much like creating a signature scent – it should reflect something personal and meaningful. Reflect on phrases that uplift or empower you, and ensure they are phrased positively.
    - When selecting a tone, think about the emotional impact of different pitches and timbres, like the difference between a warm, rich cello tone and an invigorating trumpet call, choosing one that aligns with your emotional goals.

- **Selection Criteria for Visual Anchors:**
  - Potent Visual Cues:
    - A powerful visual anchor has the allure of an iconic logo. It should be simple yet evocative, easily calling to mind the desired emotional state.
    - Consider colors and shapes that resonate with you the way a familiar

landscape or cherished artwork does, triggering feelings of peace, joy, or motivation.

- Creating Visual Reminders:
- Step-by-step, build your visual anchor by selecting evocative images or items, much like curating a gallery of art that speaks to your soul.
- Place these visual cues in strategic locations where you will encounter them during moments you most need that emotional boost, akin to strategically positioning road signs for guidance on a journey.

- **<u>Combining Anchors:</u>**
- Synergy of Sensory Cues:
- Like a meal where every flavor and texture is harmoniously blended, combining auditory and visual anchors creates a more immersive experience.
- Consider how a particular sound paired with a compelling image can create a rich tapestry of stimulation, embedding the emotional state more deeply into your psyche.

- Integration into Daily Routines:
- Embed these paired anchors into daily habits as naturally as you might pair a morning stretch with a favorite song to awaken the senses.
- Regularly engage with your combined anchors in contextually relevant situations, ensuring that they are not only effective but also a seamless part of your day-to-day activities.

By layering auditory and visual anchors, like a composer skillfully combining instruments and melodies, you create a symphony of stimuli that can call forth powerful states of being, enriching your life with an array of emotional textures at your command.

To determine the effectiveness of your anchors, consider the practice of journaling or self-reflection as a means of evaluation. This is akin to reviewing performance data after a workout session: it's about observing outcomes to gauge progress. After employing an anchor, take a moment to record your emotional state and any changes you experience in your journal. Note the intensity, duration, and impact of the emotional state that follows. Be as factual and specific as possible, akin to writing a lab report, where objectivity is key.

Self-reflection, on the other hand, is more introspective, akin to a postgame analysis in sports. Set aside time to contemplate your internal responses to the anchor. Did it prompt the emotional state you anticipated? How quickly did the emotion arise? Was it as powerful as you intended? Considering these questions helps you tune into the nuances of your experiences with the anchor.

If your findings suggest that the anchor is less effective than desired, consider adjustments. This might mean selecting a more potent emotional memory or altering the physical cue. Regular, honest assessment and a willingness to recalibrate ensure that your anchors maintain their intended power, much like fine-tuning an instrument keeps it in concert pitch, ready for a symphony.

In selecting auditory anchors, consider factors such as clarity, distinctiveness, and the ability of the sound to evoke a specific emotional reaction. The cues should be as unique and personal as your favorite playlist that effortlessly changes your mood. For instance, if a certain genre of music brings back positive memories, a snippet of a song from that genre could serve as an effective auditory anchor. When choosing mantras or tones, reflect on phrases or sounds that hold a significant emotional weight for you, such as a calming phrase heard in childhood or a victory chant from a memorable event.

For visual anchors, identify images, symbols, or items that have a strong, positive association with your past experiences. These could be as simple and familiar as a family photo that brings a sense of comfort or a souvenir from a happy occasion that inspires joy each time you see it. Ensure that the visual cue is something you can encounter frequently, similar to a motivational poster placed in your workspace.

When combining auditory and visual anchors, first determine if the combination naturally aligns with the emotional state you aim to evoke. For example, pair the sound of ocean waves (auditory) with a photograph of the beach (visual) to reinforce a state of relaxation. Integrate these combined anchors into your daily life by setting up routines where both the sound and the image are present. This could mean playing your chosen piece of music while looking at your visual anchor each morning, to start your day with a specific mindset.

Consistency in this practice is key; incorporating the combined anchors into your daily activities is like developing a muscle memory that makes the desired emotional state more automatic and naturally accessible when you need it. This integration involves not only creating these anchors but also regularly evaluating and adjusting them to ensure they continue to serve you well.

Anchoring in Neuro-Linguistic Programming is a transformative technique that offers control over emotional states, potentially revolutionizing the way individuals respond to everyday situations. By establishing a link between a physical trigger and a desired emotion, one can intentionally evoke feelings such as calmness, confidence, or motivation on demand. This skill, once honed and integrated into daily routines, can significantly enhance performance, whether in high-pressure professional environments, public speaking, or personal interactions. Beyond performance, consistent use of anchoring can improve overall emotional well-being, enabling individuals to quickly shift out of negative states and into more positive ones, thereby creating a more balanced and fulfilling life experience. Given the profound benefits, mastering the art of anchoring is a worthwhile addition to anyone's personal development toolkit, in pursuit of heightened emotional agility and empowerment.

REFRAMING TRANSFORMING PERSPECTIVE

In "Reframing: Transforming Perspective," we will journey on the practical understanding of cognitive reframing. This chapter is dedicated to unraveling how slight shifts in perception can transform challenges into avenues for personal development. Reframing is not merely an abstract psychological concept; it is a readily applicable method for altering our responses to life's hurdles. The technique hinges on recognizing our automatic thoughts and deliberately modifying these internal narratives to better serve our goals and well-being. As we navigate through this chapter, we'll examine reframing's unique capacity to influence our mindset and behavior, delivering tools that can enhance resilience, adaptability, and ultimately, success.

At the heart of reframing is the understanding that our perspectives on life's events are not fixed but can be adjusted for our benefit. This concept empowers us to reinterpret negative experiences, finding constructive angles that were not immediately apparent. For instance, consider a professional setback: rather than seeing it as a failure, reframing allows us to view it as an opportunity to re-evaluate our path and identify areas for growth. When we recalibrate our viewpoint on a challenging situation, we're not changing the facts—we're changing how we interact with those facts. This shift in perspective can turn a roadblock into a detour that leads to new insights and solutions, fostering resilience and encouraging a proactive stance toward life's obstacles. Reframing isn't about painting every situation with unfounded positivity; it's about searching for authentic, positive approaches that provide a real foundation for progress.

The reframing process is a step-by-step method designed to shift your mindset about challenges or negative situations, ultimately changing your interaction with them. Here's a guide to help you navigate this transformative journey:

Step 1: Recognition - Begin by sharpening your awareness. This is like noticing the warning lights on your car's dashboard. Pay attention to when a negative mindset kicks in. It could be a sinking feeling when facing a task or a mental block against certain activities. Acknowledge this as your mind setting up a negative frame.

Step 2: Analysis - Break down your negative thoughts and feelings like a mechanic inspecting under the hood. Investigate what triggers these thoughts, their origin, and how they influence your behavior. Are they based on past experiences? Do they arise from fear of the unknown or self-doubt? Understanding these factors is crucial for the next steps.

Step 3: Generation of Alternatives - It's time to brainstorm. Like a writer drafting different storylines, think up alternative ways to view the situation. Construct narratives that cast the event in a better light or reveal the silver linings. For example, see a failed project as a learning experience rather than a disaster.

Step 4: Evaluation - Now, compare these new narratives with your original mindset. This is much like a taste test; you're checking which narrative feels more genuine and holds more promise for positive change. Does the alternative narrative lessen the emotional weight and pave the way for a more constructive approach?

Step 5: Adoption - Once you've chosen the narrative that empowers you, make it part of your mental script. Just as a pilot runs through a new flight path, begin to integrate this perspective into your daily thought process and actions. Notice how this changes your approach to challenges and increases your resilience.

By following this guide, you move from merely coping with life's setbacks to actively reshaping your experiences. This approach doesn't just help you bounce back; it sets you on a path of growth and proactive living.

Think of your daily commute: you probably travel the same roads every day, responding to traffic signals and patterns out of habit. Your mental thought patterns can be quite similar to these familiar routes. Just like you might automatically take an exit without thinking, you might react to certain life events with negative thoughts by rote. Recognizing the need for reframing is like realizing that your usual road is always congested and deciding to take a different path. Perhaps this new route offers a scenic view or a quicker way to your destination, just like reframing can provide a more positive outlook or an effective solution to what seemed like an intractable problem. This realization is vital because it's the first step in choosing to leave the gridlock of unhelpful thinking behind in favor of a clearer, more open road ahead.

Here is the breakdown on the crucial steps for recognizing and changing negative thought patterns, using familiar analogies to clarify each component:

- **<u>Identification of Patterns:</u>**
  - Key Indicators:
    - **<u>Persistent Pessimism</u>**: Like a stop sign that makes you halt, persistent pessimism is a clear indicator to stop and reflect on your thoughts.
    - **<u>Overgeneralization</u>**: If you make a single mistake and think you always fail, that's like hitting one pothole and assuming the whole road is bad.
  - Self-Observation Techniques:
    - **<u>Thought Journaling</u>**: Keeping a journal of your thoughts is like installing a dashcam. It provides a clear record of where your mind goes throughout the day.
    - **<u>Mindfulness Meditation</u>**: Practicing mindfulness is like tuning into a live traffic update. It helps you become aware of your thought patterns in real-time.

- **<u>Assessment of Thoughts:</u>**
  - Constructive vs. Destructive:
    - **<u>Alignment with Goals</u>**: Assess if a thought is construction or roadblock to your goals, much like determining if a road sign directs you to your destination or leads you in circles.
    - **<u>Emotional Impact</u>**: Notice if thoughts uplift or drain you, similar to how a smooth road can ease your drive or a bumpy one can cause discomfort.

- **<u>Development of New Routes:</u>**
  - Constructing Positive Patterns:
    - **<u>Affirmations</u>**: Use positive affirmations as new road signs to guide your thought traffic in a beneficial direction.
    - **<u>Cognitive Restructuring</u>**: This is like road construction. You're actively working to repair and rebuild the pathways of your thoughts.
  - Practice and Solidification:
    - **<u>Consistent Repetition</u>**: Just as you need to drive over a new bridge a few times to get used to it, you must regularly practice your new thought routes to make them stick.

- **Supportive Environment**: Surround yourself with positivity, like a well-maintained road with clear markings, to support and reinforce your new thought patterns.

Through this guide, you'll have a structured approach to transform your thought highways, leading you to mental destinations that are not just enjoyable but also enriching your life journey. With practice, these new routes of thinking will become second nature, providing you with a smoother, more scenic mental landscape.

Interrupting negative thought patterns begins with pinpointing the moment when a pessimistic outlook takes hold. Like slamming the brakes to avoid a hazard on the road, the first step is to stop the cycle before it spirals. Once identified, challenge these thoughts by asking yourself what evidence you have for and against them, treating the process as objectively as an auditor reviewing financial records. Next, intentionally pivot to a positive or neutral thought, much like a driver would switch lanes to bypass an obstacle. Reinforce this positive thought through repetition, embedding it in your mental circuitry; think of it as rerouting your GPS from a well-worn but problematic path to a new, more efficient one. Consistently applying these steps whenever negative thoughts occur ensures a shift away from self-defeating patterns and towards a mindset more conducive to growth and positivity. This practical approach equips you with the tools to not just address ephemural feelings but to enact lasting cognitive change.

Let's take a deeper look at the practical steps needed to effectively challenge and change negative thought patterns, breaking it down into a process as methodical as a chef preparing a gourmet meal:

- **Detection and Interruption:**
  - Mood Tracking:
    - Like a chef tastes a dish for balance, use mood tracking apps or journals to notice the 'flavor' of your thought patterns. Detect whether they are overly pessimistic or unhelpfully negative.
  - Trigger Identification:
    - Identify specific scenarios or events that consistently lead to negative thinking, much like isolating an ingredient that causes an allergic reaction.
  - Thought Interruption:
    - When you catch yourself in a spiral of negativity, use techniques such as deep breathing or saying "stop" out loud to interrupt the flow, similar to turning down the heat under a boiling pot.

- **<u>Evidence Evaluation:</u>**
  - Cognitive Distortion Recognition:
    - Review your thoughts for common distortions. Are you "catastrophizing" or "overgeneralizing"? This is like checking a recipe against trusted sources to ensure it's accurate.
  - Reality-Checking Questions:
    - Challenge your thoughts with questions like, "What evidence do I have for this?" or "Is there another way to look at this situation?" It's similar to taste-testing as you cook, adjusting the flavors to get the desired outcome.

- **<u>Thought Substitution:</u>**
  - Constructing Alternatives:
    - Develop positive counter-narratives to negative thoughts. For example, replace "I can't handle this" with "I've handled difficult situations before." It's like substituting a missing ingredient with an equally effective alternative.
  - Anchoring Positive Thoughts:
    - Use sensory cues, like a soothing aroma or a comforting texture, as reminders to shift your thinking, much like using a timer to remember when to take the next step in a recipe.

- **<u>Repetition and Reinforcement:</u>**
  - Reminders and Rituals:
    - Set up prompts in your environment to practice positive thoughts, akin to setting notification alarms for meal times.
  - Practice:
    - Regularly rehearse your new positive thoughts to make them more natural, similar to a chef perfecting a dish through repeated testing and refinement.

By following these steps, you're not just stirring the pot of your cognitive processes; you're adding the right ingredients and techniques to transform the entire meal. With patience and practice, the result is a nourishing mindset that serves you well in all life's courses.

To apply reframing strategies to your personal situations, first identify the thought you want to change. Let's say you're consistently thinking, "I never do anything right." This kind of thought can be immediately recognized as a candidate for reframing. Now, question this negative thought by comparing it to the actual evidence from your past experiences. Have there truly been no instances of success at all? Through this assessment, you're likely to find examples that refute the absolute nature of your original thought.

Next, consciously construct a new statement that is more accurate and kinder to yourself. It could be something like, "I've faced challenges before and have found ways to succeed." This statement is your reframed thought. Practice this statement; say it out loud, write it down, or repeat it in your mind, especially when you catch yourself slipping into the old pattern. Over time, with persistence, this deliberate practice will adjust your automatic response to a more balanced and fair self-assessment.

Everything from setting reminders on your phone to repeating your new perspective during daily tasks like brushing your teeth can help cement this reframed thought. Similar to training for a sport or learning a new language, the key is repetition and consistency—this is how your brain forms new habits. As these new thoughts become habitual, they'll begin to shape your behavior and reactions, leading to a more positive viewpoint on your actions and yourself.

Let's take a deeper look at the nuances of swapping out negative thoughts for positive ones like a gardener who not only removes weeds but also plants seeds that will grow into a vibrant garden:

- **Identification of Barriers:**
- Address emotional resistance, which could manifest as a discomfort or a feeling that the positive thoughts are insincere — it's like trying to plant in unyielding soil.
- Recognize that change generally doesn't happen overnight. Patience here is as important as it is for a gardener waiting for seeds to germinate.

- **In-depth Questioning Techniques:**
- Ask, "What past experiences are causing this thought?" This is akin to tracing a vine back to its roots to understand where it's coming from.
- Pose the question, "Is this thought based on facts or feelings?" separating the nutrient-rich soil of reality from the rocks of misconception.

- **Developing and Integrating Replacement Thoughts:**

- Craft positive thoughts that resonate with your core values, much like selecting plants that will thrive in your garden's unique conditions.
- Incorporate these thoughts using visualization, picturing the success they will bring as clearly as a gardener visualizes a full bloom. Pair them with body movement, like a deep breath, to create a multi-sensory link.

- **<u>Monitoring and Adjusting:</u>**
- Keep a journal of your thought patterns, akin to a garden diary. Note what works and what doesn't, and be ready to prune away tactics that aren't helping your mindset flourish.
- Set regular intervals to review this journal, making adjustments as needed, just as a gardener would regularly check on their plants and soil.

This approach, rich in detail and care, will set you on a path not just to weed out negative thoughts, but to cultivate a mindset abundant with positive, life-affirming beliefs.

Applying reframing techniques in your daily life can be much like editing a photograph on your phone. When you take a picture, sometimes the lighting isn't right, or the angle doesn't showcase the subject as you'd hoped. With a few simple adjustments, you can transform the image into one that's more pleasing. Reframing your thoughts works similarly. You might encounter a situation that seems negative at first glance—like a snapshot marred by shadows. But with reframing, you can adjust the 'contrast' of your perception, highlighting the positives and dimming the negative aspects. Just as you might crop out unwanted parts of a photo to focus on the best elements, you can choose to concentrate on the aspects of a situation that empower you, discarding unnecessary negative details. This practice doesn't require complex skills; a little bit of awareness and some tweaks to your mindset can turn an ordinary scene into an extraordinary one, changing how you view and react to everyday life.

Here is the breakdown on the reframing process, laid out like a series of steps to upgrade your mental picture gallery:

- **<u>Identifying the need for reframing</u>:**
- **<u>Persistent negativity</u>**: Recognize when there's a pattern of negative thinking, like the same cloudy weather that obscures the view day after day.
- **<u>Emotional discomfort</u>**: Notice feelings of distress or frustration that are frequently connected to specific thoughts, signaling the need for a

mindset 'climate change'.

- **<u>Techniques for capturing the 'photo' of your current thought pattern</u>**:
- **<u>Journaling</u>**: Write down your thoughts regularly as if you're keeping a photo journal of your mind. This helps you see the 'scenes' you often return to.
- **<u>Mindfulness Reflection</u>**: Pause at different times of the day to introspect, like taking a snapshot of your feelings and thoughts, bringing awareness to recurrent patterns.

- **<u>Adjusting the 'settings'</u>**:
- **<u>Positive affirmation</u>**: Practice this like increasing the brightness to enhance the best parts of your mental picture.
- **<u>Gratitude exercises</u>**: Focus on things you're grateful for as if they're the vibrant colors that make your picture pop.

- **<u>Cropping out the unhelpful</u>**:
- **<u>Selective focus</u>**: Learn to zoom in on constructive thoughts and let the background of negativity blur away.
- **<u>Challenge and replace</u>**: Actively replace unhelpful thoughts with beneficial ones, much like choosing which elements stay in the frame of your picture.

- **<u>Maintaining the 'Edited Album'</u>**:
- **<u>Regular Review</u>**: Frequently go over your new thought patterns, like a photographer reviewing their portfolio, to ensure quality remains high.
- **<u>Mindfulness Practice</u>**: Integrate steady mindfulness habits to keep the album of positive thoughts in clear view, like keeping a treasured album on the coffee table for easy access.

Each step in this process is a move towards a richer, more balanced collection of mental 'photos' that represent a more fulfilling life narrative. With attention and practice, you'll be able to curate a mindset gallery that truly reflects your capabilities and aspirations.

J.K. Rowling's journey to writing the Harry Potter series is a classic case of reframing in action. Picture her initial manuscript rejections not as stop signs but as redirections on her path to success. Each "no" could have been a boulder blocking her way, but she chose to see them as stepping stones, guiding her to improve and persevere. This mindset shift—seeing rejection as refinement—propelled her narrative from struggling writer to one of the most successful authors of our time.

In a similar vein, Thomas Edison's experience in inventing the lightbulb showcases reframing on a grand scale. He famously regarded his numerous failed attempts not as failures but as discoveries of ways that did not work, a clear example of reimagining setbacks as progress. Instead of a pile of mistakes to be discarded, each unsuccessful experiment was a crucial clue in his investigative process, ultimately leading to a world-changing invention.

Both Rowling and Edison exemplify how altering our internal script around setbacks can redefine the stories of our lives, turning potential tales of surrender into epics of triumph. They remind us that the narrative of success is often written by those who learn to read failure through a different lens.

Here is the breakdown on the specific reframing techniques and thought processes that icons like J.K. Rowling and Thomas Edison might have used to navigate through their challenges:

- **<u>Mental Shifts and Emotional Strategies</u>**:
    - Building Resilience:
    - Rowling could have embraced each rejection as proof of her commitment, much like collecting stamps on a passport, each one marking a step toward her destination.
    - Edison might have celebrated each failed experiment as a 'successful elimination' of an ineffective solution, seeing progress where others saw stagnation.
    - Maintaining Motivation:
    - Both may have used visualization techniques, imagining the success of their endeavors as vividly as a painter visualizes the finished canvas long before the brush touches paint.
    - Positive self-talk could have been a daily ritual, perhaps repeating mantras such as "Every no brings me closer to yes," or "I haven't failed; I've found another way that doesn't work," using words to reinforce their unshakable belief in their goals.

- **Iterative Development**:
  - Learning from Feedback:
  - Rowling's revisions in response to publisher feedback might have been as careful and deliberate as an artist tweaking brushstrokes to perfect a painting.
  - Edison's approach to each new prototype could be likened to a chef who tweaks a recipe batch after batch, undeterred by a dish that doesn't come out right the first time.

- **Long-Term Vision Maintenance**:
  - Staying the Course:
  - They probably anchored their daily tasks to their larger visions, just as a captain keeps a ship on course by frequently checking the compass and adjusting the sails.
  - By consciously linking each small action and decision to the end goal, they ensured that their thought patterns and focus remained aligned, treating every obstacle as a puzzle piece rather than a full stop.

This in-depth exploration reveals the inner workings behind the continued drive and problem-solving mindset of people who have reframed potential failures into lessons and stepping stones to success. It's a process of internal negotiation and perspective-shift that mirrors the trials and tribulations faced by many in the pursuit of remarkable achievements.

Imagine you're working on a team project and suddenly, you're assigned a challenging task or facing a tight deadline. In the throes of stress, you might see this as an unwelcome burden. Reframing here means viewing the challenge not as a roadblock but as an opportunity to showcase your skills or learn new ones—much like a gamer encountering a new level, it's a chance to level up. Or perhaps there's a colleague you often clash with. Through the lens of reframing, this isn't a thorn in your side; rather, it's a chance to develop patience and understanding, akin to a tricky puzzle that, once solved, makes you sharper.

In interpersonal relationships, consider a disagreement with a friend or partner. Instead of dwelling on the conflict, reframe it as a conversation that deepens your understanding of each other, much like pruning a plant to encourage healthier growth. Reframing doesn't dismiss the difficulty of these situations; it simply shifts the focus to the positive outcomes and growth they can engender. It's a subtle change in perspective that can transform obstacles into stepping stones, turning everyday challenges into invaluable experiences.

Let's take a deeper look at the strategies that J.K. Rowling and Thomas Edison might have used as they broke through their respective challenges, each component showcasing the resilience and tenacity needed for their monumental achievements:

- **<u>Mental Shifts and Emotional Strategies</u>**:
   - Nurturing Resilience:
   - Rowling could have fostered a 'shield' of positive reinforcement around her writing, viewing each rejection not as a sword against her work but as armor bolstering her for the next round.
   - Edison might have perceived his failures as a scientist's experiments, each one not a dent in his confidence but a step closer to the right formula.
   - Motivation Maintenance:
   - They both could have employed mental cue cards, like personal affirmations or visualization of the end goal, keeping their aspirations clearly in sight, much like bookmarks that remind readers where the story is headed.

- **<u>Iterative Development</u>**:
   - Learning from Setbacks:
   - Each "no" received by Rowling could have been seen as a test review session, where the feedback is not a grade but guidance for improvement.
   - Edison's failed lightbulb prototypes might have been like puzzle pieces, which were not misfits but rather clues well-suited for different parts of a larger picture.

- **<u>Long-Term Vision Maintenance</u>**:
   - Strategic Focus:
   - In maintaining their long-term visions despite the hurdles, Rowling and Edison would have had to master the art of 'perspective zooming,' focusing on the close-up work at hand while ensuring it fit into the bigger picture they envisioned.

Through these approaches, both Rowling and Edison transformed barriers into bridges, illustrating not just the power of a single reframing technique but the impact of a reframed mindset on life's grand canvas. The narratives of their lives demonstrate how seeing beyond momentary impediments and embracing each step as necessary for growth can sculpt unremarkable beginnings into legendary success stories.

To build the habit of reframing into your daily routine, treat it as you would any essential part of your health regimen. Begin with setting a clear intention: just as you would decide which vitamin to take or what exercise to do, choose a specific area of your thought patterns that you want to work on. Maybe it's your tendency to view all workplace feedback as criticism instead of opportunities for growth.

Once you've identified the target, establish triggers that remind you to engage in reframing, similar to setting out your running shoes the night before. These could be alarms on your phone or sticky notes in places you frequently look, reminding you to shift your perspective.

When a trigger occurs, practice the reframing: counter a negative thought with a positive reinterpretation, just as you might choose an apple over a cookie. Provide yourself with ready-to-go, constructive alternative thoughts.

Reinforce this new habit by reflecting on its benefits at the end of the day. Acknowledge any progress you've made, as you would after a week of healthy eating, and make note of how your new perspective has shaped your experiences.

Keep track of your journey to make reframing a habit—note successes and moments when old patterns reemerged, much like you'd record your meals or workouts. Adjust your approach as needed, staying flexible and patient with your progress. Over time, with consistency, reframing will become a natural part of your mental toolkit, fostering a healthier, more positive mindset.

To truly integrate the habit of reframing into your daily life and ensure it sticks, let's break down the approach into practical, actionable steps.

First, consider your internal motivators. Pinpoint the values and long-term objectives that matter most to you. Maybe it's becoming a better problem-solver to excel at work or maintaining healthier relationships. Connecting your reframing practice to these deeper aspirations can be a powerful way to fuel your commitment. It's like selecting a fitness goal that resonates with you personally, rather than following someone else's routine.

In terms of habit formation, the psychological trifecta of cues, routines, and rewards is crucial. Set clear, specific cues for yourself – like placing your journal next to your morning coffee as a reminder to write down one thing you'll reframe each day. Establish routines by consistently following through on these cues – perhaps you'll write down negative thoughts as they occur and pivot to a positive angle immediately. Finally, reward yourself for engaging in this new habit. This could be a small treat, like allowing yourself an episode of your favorite show after a week of consistent reframing.

When you hit a wall and your motivation wavers, have a plan ready. For example, if something disrupts your routine and you miss a reframing session, schedule a make-up session rather than letting one slip-up derail your progress. A support system can also be invaluable. Share your reframing goals with a trusted friend or family member who can help encourage you.

And don't underestimate the power of digital helpers. Tools and apps designed for habit tracking can serve as your personal accountability partners, reminding you when it's time to engage in reframing and allowing you to visualize your progress over time.

Implementing these tips will help you develop a robust reframing routine, transforming this practice into a natural part of your mental wellness just as brushing your teeth is a cornerstone of your physical hygiene.

Reframing is more than just a mental trick; it's a powerful tool that can redefine how we approach life's challenges and interpret our experiences. By learning and applying this technique, we open the door to a world where obstacles become opportunities for learning, and setbacks transform into stepping stones for growth. It encourages us to move beyond our immediate reactions and consider alternatives that can lead to more positive outcomes. Embracing reframing is essentially giving ourselves a lens that brings resilience and adaptability into focus, two qualities that are invaluable in both personal development and professional advancement. As you continue to navigate through your life journey, remember the potential of reframing to change not just your thoughts, but the very trajectory of your story.

STRATEGIES PROGRAMMING SUCCESS

Neuro-Linguistic Programming (NLP) encapsulates key principles that serve as a blueprint for effective communication and personal development. At its core, NLP rests on the idea that language and thought patterns are intimately connected to behavior, much like gears in a clockwork influencing the movement of hands. One principle is representational systems, the concept that individuals process information through sensory channels - seeing, hearing, feeling, tasting, and smelling. By tuning into a person's preferred system, communication can become more targeted and persuasive.

Another central tenet is the use of meta-models, linguistic tools that challenge and expand the limits of one's personal experiences. These tools clarify speech by asking precise questions, breaking down vague language, much like a microscope reveals details invisible to the naked eye.

NLP also emphasizes the importance of outcome thinking, a process of defining and focusing on desired results. Think of it as setting a destination in a navigation system; clearly specifying where you want to go increases the chances of appropriately directing your efforts to get there.

By leveraging these principles, individuals can pave the way towards improved interactions and personal achievements. A comprehensive understanding of NLP's mechanisms enables one to recalibrate their internal dialogue, reshape their understanding of experiences, and rewire their response patterns, leading to more consciously chosen and fruitful outcomes in various aspects of life.

Let's take a deeper look at how NLP's representational systems can be applied for more effective communication. Each system - visual, auditory, kinesthetic, olfactory, and gustatory - processes information in a distinct way, similar to how different instruments create unique sounds in an orchestra.

- **<u>Visual:</u>** If a person often uses phrases like "I see your point" or "Let's look at it another way," they may have a visual style. You can engage them by painting pictures with words, using descriptions that invoke images, akin to discussing the vivid colors and shapes in a painting.

- **Auditory:** Someone with an auditory preference might say, "That sounds right to me" or "I hear you loud and clear." To resonate with them, employ rhythmic language and adjust your tone and pitch, much like tuning a radio to the listener's favorite station.

- **Kinesthetic:** Indicators of a kinesthetic communicator include statements like "I need to get a grip on this" or "That doesn't sit right with me." Engage their tactile senses by discussing textures and feelings, as though inviting them to feel the weight and texture of a fabric.

- **Olfactory and Gustatory:** These are less common but no less important. A person keen on these senses may describe experiences with "This situation stinks" or "That idea left a bad taste in my mouth." To connect, mention scents and tastes when appropriate, drawing parallels with the aroma of freshly baked bread or the tartness of lemon.

Adjusting your language to align with someone's dominant system can drastically enhance your communication. Imagine you're trying to persuade a visual person to join your project. Describe your vision in picturesque detail, talk about how it "looks," and ensure your collateral, like slides or handouts, are visually engaging.

In daily life, if you're wanting to comfort a kinesthetic friend, opt for a warm hug or a pat on the back instead of just verbal assurances, tapping directly into their need for physical comfort.

By tailoring your approach to match the specific sensory preferences of those you're communicating with, you can increase rapport, understanding, and overall impact. Think of it as choosing the right key to unlock a door, granting you access to more meaningful and influential interactions.

Imagine you're in the kitchen of a master chef, watching attentively as they craft their signature dish. With each precise chop, carefully measured ingredient, and perfected technique, they're not just making a meal, they're sharing a blueprint for culinary excellence. NLP modeling works much like this culinary transmission of secrets. It's about identifying the 'recipes' for success used by those who excel in their field.

The first step is observation. Just as you'd study how the chef selects their ingredients, you observe the successful individual, noting their behaviors, language, and thought processes. Then comes imitation, trying out each 'ingredient' and 'technique' yourself — replicating their actions and adopting their mindset.

As you become more familiar with the recipe, you start to tweak it to fit your own tastes, skills, and circumstances. If the chef uses thyme and you prefer rosemary, you make the substitution. Similarly, in NLP modeling, you adapt the behaviors and attitudes to better suit your personal goals and style.

Finally, with practice, the dish — or in the case of NLP, the modeled strategies — become second nature. You can whip up the dish without the recipe, just as you can embody the success strategies without constant conscious thought. This process allows you to internalize the very patterns that lead to success, making them part of your own repertoire. It's about taking what works from others' experiences and cooking up your own version of success in the kitchen of life.

Setting goals with NLP is akin to captaining a ship on a voyage toward uncharted waters. Just as a skilled navigator sets the course using a map, marks the compass direction, and charts out the marine paths to follow, NLP helps you define clear objectives and a detailed route to your destination. Imagine you're the captain at the helm, you wouldn't just plot a course; you'd also prepare for potential storms and adjust for the currents.

In NLP, this translates to anticipating challenges and remaining flexible enough to adjust your strategies as conditions change. You start with a vision of your destination, a clear image of success that guides all decisions, just as a lighthouse provides a point of reference for safe harbor. Then, you map out specific milestones along the way, ensuring your journey has structure and measurable progress—like checkpoints across the ocean.

Finally, similar to how a ship's crew is essential for a smooth expedition, surrounding yourself with a supportive network can be crucial in keeping you on course. NLP goal-setting isn't about sailing blindly into the fog but navigating with intention, precision, and preparedness, ensuring that every action moves you closer to your aspiration shore.

Here is the breakdown of the NLP goal-setting process, charting a course for success with clarity and precision:

- **<u>Identify Clear Objectives:</u>**
  - Craft a vivid and specific description of your goal, akin to a captain knowing the destination port.
  - Detail what success looks like, feels like, and even sounds like, using sensory-rich language.
  - Reflect on why this goal is important to you, as this is your compass that keeps you oriented.

- **<u>Map Out a Route with Key Milestones:</u>**
  - Divide the journey to your goal into smaller, manageable segments— each milestone a nautical marker along your path.
  - Define these milestones with clear indicators of progress, setting timelines as you would estimate travel times at sea.

- **<u>Anticipate and Prepare for Challenges:</u>**
  - List possible setbacks or obstacles you might encounter, just as a captain anticipates weather changes.
  - Develop contingency plans for each obstacle, equipping your 'ship' with the needed resources and knowledge to navigate through rough conditions.

- **<u>Flexibility and Adaptation:</u>**
  - Stay open to adjusting your strategies, much like sailors adapt to wind and tide shifts, to progress towards your goal despite changing circumstances.
  - Regularly reassess your progress and methods, staying agile and responsive, always ready to alter the sails to catch the best wind.

- **<u>Build and Leverage a Supportive Network:</u>**
  - Identify individuals who can offer guidance, support, and insight,

viewing them as your crew, each with a vital role in the voyage.

- Engage with mentors, peers, and confidants who can encourage and assist you, maintaining open lines of communication as you would with a team navigating a ship.

By anchoring these steps in the familiar process of maritime navigation, the goal-setting journey through NLP becomes not a solitary drift but a purposeful, well-navigated quest. Each step, from setting the destination to reaching new ports of call, becomes an integral part of a grander voyage — the pursuit of your personal and professional aspirations.

Reframing in NLP is the process of viewing a situation, thought, or feeling from a different perspective; it's like looking at an old picture in a new frame, causing a shift in how it's perceived. It begins with identifying the negative belief that's acting like an anchor, holding you back. Once pinpointed, you deliberately challenge this belief by examining evidence for and against it, asking yourself more empowering questions, and replacing it with a positive or neutral belief.

Anchoring, on the other hand, involves creating an association between a specific stimulus and a desired emotional state. It's similar to hearing a song that instantly transports you back to a memorable moment. To form an anchor, you first get into a state where you feel the emotion you want to capture. Then, at the peak of this feeling, apply a unique stimulus, like a touch on your hand. Repeating this technique strengthens the link, so when you need to elicit this emotion in the future, you can use the stimulus like pushing a button on a control panel to adjust your emotional sails.

Employing these two techniques helps navigate through the mental fog into clearer, calmer waters. By reframing thoughts and planting positive emotional anchors, you essentially set courses for more productive destinations, keeping you buoyant even amidst life's undulating tides.

Step 1: Start by pinpointing exactly what the negative thought or belief is. Write it down in detail, just as if you were recording symptoms for a doctor. Be as specific as possible about the context in which it occurs and the feelings it evokes.

Step 2: Challenge this belief by engaging in a mental cross-examination.

Ask yourself questions like, "What evidence do I have that supports this belief?", "Is this belief always true, in every situation?", and "How would I view this situation if I had a more positive belief?" These are like mental spotlights uncovering the shadows where doubts reside.

Step 3: Select a stimulus for anchoring that is unique and can be easily replicated by you at any time. It could be a touch on the wrist, a specific word or gesture, or even a unique scent. The key is consistency and relevance – like choosing a distinctive ringtone for an important caller.

Step 4: Induce the desired emotional state through a memory or visualization that reliably triggers that emotion. Once fully immersed in this feeling, activate your chosen stimulus. This is like bookmarking a favorite page in a book so you can quickly return to it.

Step 5: Strengthen the anchor by repeating the association. Every time you experience the positive emotion, apply the stimulus. Do this multiple times until the connection is automatic, just as a catchy song chorus that immediately starts playing in your head when you hear the first few notes.

Step 6: If the anchor doesn't seem to work, reconsider your chosen stimulus – maybe it's not distinctive enough, or it doesn't fit the context of the emotional state. Similarly, if reframing a belief isn't sticking, ensure you're not overly attached to the negative belief due to some secondary gain. Persevere with interrogating the belief and seek counterexamples to establish a more positive outlook. Just like troubleshooting a faulty engine – if one approach fails, try another until you find the right solution.

Remember, NLP is a practical toolbox. Like any skill, it requires practice and application. With patience and persistence, your efforts can lead to meaningful change and enhanced control over your mental and emotional landscape.

One notable application of Neuro-Linguistic Programming can be observed in the preparation process of a public speaker. Take, for instance, a speaker gearing up for a TED Talk. They might use NLP techniques, such as modeling, to harness the stage prowess of acclaimed speakers. They watch videos, dissect speech patterns, and emulate body language to cultivate a powerful presence. Mental rehearsal, another NLP strategy, allows them to vividly visualize delivering the talk with poise and confidence, reinforcing a successful performance in their mind before setting foot on stage.

Therapists often leverage NLP to assist clients in overcoming phobias. They use anchoring to associate a client's calm and relaxed state with a specific touch or gesture. This anchor is then called upon when the client confronts the phobic stimulus, enabling them to access feelings of tranquility in the face of fear. Reframing is also common, helping clients view their phobia from a new perspective, detaching the automatic fear response from the object of their phobia.

These examples demystify NLP's application, demonstrating how it can be a powerful changemaker in both personal development and assisting others. By understanding these strategies in straightforward, actionable terms, we see how NLP serves as more than just a theoretical framework; it offers practical utilities that can produce tangible improvements in various aspects of life.

Let's take a deeper look at the specific steps a public speaker would follow using NLP techniques to prepare for a talk:

For modeling:
- First, choose a speaker who represents the kind of success you aspire to. This might be someone you admire for their confidence, rapport with the audience, or eloquent delivery.
- Study recordings of their performances. Pay close attention to how they open their talk, the gestures they use for emphasis, the pace and variations in their voice, and how they conclude.
- Practicing emulation entails breaking down these observations into actionable steps. You might start by rehearsing your speech with similar intonations or adopting some of their signature movements that resonate with you. It's like trying on a tailored suit and adjusting it until it fits you perfectly.

Regarding mental rehearsal:
- Picture the venue where you'll be speaking. Imagine stepping onto the stage, facing the crowd, feeling the lights on your skin. Incorporate the sound of your voice echoing through the room and the sense of satisfaction as you

articulate your words.

- Rehearse this imagery regularly, especially during moments of calm, so the positive emotions become anchored to the experience. It's like running a race in your mind before the starting gun fires, so you're ready for victory.

For a therapist helping clients with phobias:
- To set anchors, find a moment when the client is truly at ease. It could be as simple as guiding them through breathing exercises to achieve this state.
- Introduce a unique stimulus, like a gentle squeeze of the hand, at the peak of their relaxation. Reinforce this through repetition in different sessions, solidifying their mental association between the touch and the calm state.
- Reframing involves conversations where the therapist helps the client view their fear differently, diminishing its impact. Rather than a giant wave threatening to plunge them underwater, the phobia could be reframed as a navigable swell on the ocean, approached with the right vessel—effective coping strategies.

Breaking down these techniques into their smallest components allows for a deeper understanding of how to implement NLP in very practical ways. Whether you're addressing an auditorium or helping someone face their fears, these strategies can anchor success in the subconscious, enabling remarkable transformations.

Integrating NLP techniques into your everyday life can be likened to learning a new language. Just as you would practice new words daily to achieve fluency, consistently applying NLP principles like reframing negative thoughts or setting anchors cultivates a new way of thinking. It's not about occasional practice, but rather about incorporating these methods into your regular activities. Much like repeating phrases in a foreign language to order food or ask for directions becomes second nature, so too does using NLP techniques like powerful questioning to enhance communication or visualization to prime yourself for success before a major event.

Listening, an essential part of language learning, parallels tuning into cues that can trigger anchors or signal opportunities for reframing in real-time conversations. Speaking, on the other hand, reflects the active use of language; similarly, consciously employing positive language patterns shapes your internal dialogue and interactions with others. This conscious practice strengthens your 'NLP muscle', embedding its principles deeply into your neural pathways, much like daily conversations reinforce language skills.

Over time, these small but significant applications of NLP become part of the fabric of your life, guiding you towards better outcomes almost automatically, like effortlessly switching between languages based on your listeners. The resulting blend of awareness and habitual practice transforms NLP from a set of exercises to a fundamental aspect of your mental toolkit, as natural as speaking your mother tongue.

Here is the breakdown on integrating NLP techniques into everyday activities:

- **While Commuting:**
    - Reframing Thoughts:
    - Identify a recurring negative thought, perhaps related to the stress of traffic or public transportation.
    - Challenge this thought by asking, "What's another way to view this situation?"
    - Replace it with a positive or productive thought, such as appreciating the time to listen to a podcast or music.

- **Before a Meeting:**
    - Using Anchoring:
    - Choose a physical action, like pressing your thumb and forefinger together.
    - Think back to a time when you felt particularly confident and recreate those emotions as vividly as possible.
    - At the height of these feelings, perform the chosen action to anchor the emotion.
    - Use this anchor right before entering a meeting to invoke confidence.

- **During Interpersonal Interactions:**
    - Practicing Powerful Questioning:
    - Engage with others by asking open-ended questions that encourage deeper thinking and dialogue.
    - For example, instead of asking, "Did you like the presentation?" ask, "What stood out to you in the presentation and why?"

- **<u>When Faced with Challenges:</u>**
    - Engaging in Positive Self-talk:
    - Confront negative self-talk by immediately stopping and reframing the language.
    - Turn "I can't handle this" into "I've handled tough situations before; I can learn from this one."

- **<u>Throughout the Day:</u>**
    - Recognizing and Utilizing Cues:
    - Pay attention to physical responses to stress or anxiety, such as a tightness in your chest or clenching your jaw.
    - Use these cues as triggers to practice breathing exercises combined with positive affirmations.

By embracing these techniques in day-to-day life, you can slowly shift your habitual responses towards more empowering and positive outcomes. It's like adding spices to your cooking; initially, you need to measure and think about each one, but over time, it becomes second nature to create meals that are perfectly seasoned to your taste. Similarly, with practice, NLP techniques can seamlessly become part of your everyday pattern, seasoning your experiences with a more positive and constructive flavor.

Neuro-Linguistic Programming, NLP, emerges as a versatile toolset with the potential to reshape personal and professional landscapes. As we've discovered, by mastering its principles and techniques—modeling, reframing, anchoring—you develop skills that can positively transform your communications, behaviors, and thought processes. It's this array of strategies that acts as a compass, guiding you through the complexities of daily life towards more successful and fulfilling outcomes. With consistent practice and application, NLP equips you with the means to navigate effectively through challenges, catalyzing personal growth and empowering you to pursue and achieve your desired goals.

INTEGRATION BRINGING IT ALL TOGETHER

It's time to talk about integration. Neuro-Linguistic Programming, or NLP, rests on a foundation of several core tenets, each playing a distinctive role in its practice. One foundational concept is that our subjective perception of the world shapes our reality, suggesting that how we interpret events is crucial to our experience. This idea is akin to wearing tinted glasses that color everything we see; by understanding this, we can change our 'lenses' and thus our experience of the world.

Another key tenet is the belief in the power of language as a tool for influencing thought and behavior. Just as a computer programmer uses code to alter software, we can use specific language patterns to program our minds for positive change.

The third principle involves modeling the success of others. This is similar to following a recipe that's been proven to yield a delicious meal; in NLP, we replicate the 'recipes' of successful behaviors and mindsets to achieve our goals.

Each of these principles contributes to the overarching purpose of NLP: to provide a strategic framework for self-improvement and effective communication. By dissecting these principles into achievable strategies, NLP empowers us to systematically enhance various aspects of our personal and professional lives. It's a pragmatic approach that combines insights from psychology and linguistics, offering a blueprint for tapping into the potential of our mind. As we explore these NLP principles further, we'll reveal how to leverage them to catalyze profound growth and change.

Applying the foundational principles of Neuro-Linguistic Programming (NLP) in everyday life can significantly enhance personal and professional growth. Here is a step-by-step guide:

<u>Perception Reevaluation:</u>

1. Recognize Your Filters: Begin by understanding that everyone has mental 'filters' that shape our perception. These are formed by your personal experiences, culture, and beliefs.

2. Challenge Assumptions: When faced with a situation, actively question your immediate response. Why do you feel a certain way? Is your reaction based on facts or preconceived notions?

3. Mindfulness Practice: Incorporate mindfulness exercises into your daily routine. Spend a few minutes each day observing your thoughts without judgment to increase awareness of your mental 'lenses'.

Language for Influence:

1. Positive Language Use: Start by changing negatives into positives in your speech. Instead of saying "don't forget," try "remember to."

2. Refining Questions: Instead of asking "Why does this always happen to me?" rephrase the question to "What can I learn from this experience?"

3. Anchoring Statements: Use powerful, affirming language to anchor positive states. Phrases like "I am capable" or "I can handle this" can reset your mindset during challenges.

4. Listening and Mirroring: In conversations, listen actively and mirror the positive language and tonality of others to strengthen rapport and communication.

Success Modeling:

1. Identify Role Models: Choose individuals who embody the success you seek. They could be colleagues, public figures, or historical personalities.

2. Observe and Note: Closely observe the behaviors, attitudes, and routines of these role models. What habits contribute to their success?

3. Implement and Personalize: Try incorporating their successful habits into your life, one at a time. Personalize these habits to fit your context and needs.

4. Review and Adjust: Regularly assess the impact of these changes. Keep what works and tweak or discard what doesn't.

Each step builds upon the last and together forms a comprehensive approach to integrating the principles of NLP into your life. Remember, the key to success with NLP is consistency and willingness to adapt as you learn. With each day, aim to deepen your understanding and refine your application of these techniques for continued personal and professional development.

Foundational NLP principles, when viewed through the lens of common experiences, can seem as familiar as the daily rituals we all engage in. Consider the principle of subjective experience—how we each view the world through our unique lens. It's like dining at a buffet; every person fills their plate based on personal taste and hunger. Our choices are based on our perceptions of what looks appetizing and what does not. Just as we can return to the buffet to adjust our selections, we can revisit and adjust our perspectives as we gain new information and experiences.

Language's role in influencing thought and behavior is another powerful NLP tenet. It's akin to a gardener tending to plants; the words we use are like water and sunlight, nurturing and shaping the growth of our thoughts. Just as a gardener selects the proper nutrients for each plant, we can cultivate our mental landscapes by choosing words that foster positive growth.

Finally, think about the NLP principle of modeling successful behaviors—similar to learning a new sport by watching and imitating a professional athlete. We see their techniques, practice replicating their movements, and gradually, through trial and improvement, we develop our own style while incorporating their expertise.

These analogies highlight how NLP principles operate in contexts we're already acquainted with, making the leap to applying them in our lives seem less like venturing into unknown territory and more like exploring a new area in our neighborhood. The natural process of adapting these principles isn't just practical; it's an expansion of practices we're already familiar with, showcasing the intrinsic value they hold for enhancing our daily lives.

Here is the breakdown on how to use the buffet analogy to tune your perception with NLP, offering a plateful of insights:

- **Initial Self-Assessment**:
  - **Identifying Personal Beliefs**:
    - First, take stock of what you currently believe about a specific situation. It's like scanning the buffet and noting your gut reaction to each dish based on what you normally eat.
  - **Recognizing Belief Origins**:
    - Consider why you hold these beliefs. Like family recipes passed down, acknowledge that your culture and past experiences flavor your perception.

- **<u>Selection of Perspectives</u>**:
  - **<u>Exploring Alternatives</u>**:
    - Make an effort to consider different angles, just as you might try a new dish at a buffet that you wouldn't typically choose.
  - **<u>Seeking New Information</u>**:
    - Actively look for fresh insights and data that challenge your habitual choices, akin to reading up on the ingredients in unfamiliar dishes to make a more informed decision.

- **<u>Adjustments and Reevaluation</u>**:
  - **<u>Integrating New Data</u>**:
    - After acquiring new information, mix it into your thinking and see how it alters your perception. It's similar to adding a new seasoning to your meal and discovering it enhances the flavor.
  - **<u>Assessing Alignment</u>**:
    - Evaluate whether this updated perspective sits well with you, aligning better with reality, much like deciding if the new food choice has enriched your dining experience.

This structured, reflective process mirrors the routine of selecting food at a buffet and allows you to reshuffle your mental menu. It's about sampling varied thoughts, digesting new ideas, and acquiring a taste for perspectives that might better suit your appetite for life. It's not just about what's on your plate but appreciating the entire spread of possibilities before you.

Creating your own NLP strategies is like charting a unique course for a personal voyage. First, pinpoint your departure point by identifying your current mindset and behavioral patterns. Just as you would assess your location before a trip, understand where you stand mentally and emotionally. Next, determine your destination: what is the change or outcome you're aiming to achieve? Set clear, measurable goals that serve as your roadmap's endpoints.

Now, plan your route by choosing which NLP techniques will guide you to your desired outcome. Perhaps you'll use the 'swish pattern' to swap a bad habit for a good one, or employ 'anchoring' to summon confidence before big meetings. As with a journey, not all roads are equally smooth or direct, so be prepared to adjust your techniques as you learn what works best for you.

As you progress, periodically check your bearings. Reflect on the effectiveness of your strategies, and don't hesitate to recalibrate if you veer off course. This step is akin to a traveler consulting their GPS and road signs, ensuring they're still on the path to their chosen destination.

Continue this process, and you'll not only reach your goals but also gain a deeper understanding of the NLP landscape and how to navigate it. This ongoing practice of personal strategy development isn't a one-off venture but a dynamic, continual growth journey that becomes more intuitive over time.

Let's take a deeper look at constructing a personalized NLP strategy for self-improvement — like mapping out a fitness routine that caters to your unique physiology.

- **<u>Goal Definition</u>**:
  - **<u>Identifying Your Ambitions</u>**: Just as a GPS needs a specific address to guide you, start by outlining what you want to achieve in clear, precise terms. This could be improving communication skills or managing stress more effectively.
  - **<u>Crafting SMART Goals</u>**: Make your goals SMART — as if you're setting the rules for a board game where winning means achieving your aims. Each goal should be Specific, Measurable, Achievable, Relevant, and Time-bound to keep track of your progress accurately.

- **<u>Technique Selection</u>**:
  - **<u>Analyzing NLP Techniques</u>**: NLP offers a toolkit much like a set of paints for an artist. Each color — or technique — can create a different effect. The 'swish pattern' can change unwanted habits, 'anchoring' can trigger desired emotional states, and 'reframing' can shift perspectives on challenging situations.
  - **<u>Matching Techniques to Needs</u>**: Choose your techniques based on personal relevance, like picking out the right attire for a specific occasion. If stress is an issue, 'anchoring' may help you summon calmness quickly; if negative self-talk is a hurdle, 'reframing' can turn self-criticism into constructive dialogue.

- **<u>Strategy Implementation</u>**:
  - **<u>Applying Techniques in Real Life</u>**: Implement the chosen

techniques as part of your routine, much as you integrate new habits like daily walks or meditation. It may take some practice, so be patient and persistent.

- **Being Adaptive**: Stay flexible in your approach. Just as you might take a detour when a road is closed, be willing to adjust your NLP techniques when they're not fitting your needs or if circumstances change.

- **Progress Monitoring**:

- **Keep a Journal**: Record your experiences like a scientist jotting down experiment notes. Note what's working, what's not, and any new patterns or insights that emerge.

- **Seek Feedback**: Reach out to trusted friends or mentors for feedback on your growth, similar to seeking restaurant recommendations to ensure a delightful dining experience.

This process is about blending the science of NLP with the art of personal development. By breaking down each step and using relatable examples, we can see how utilizing NLP strategies becomes a powerful conduit for change, much like learning to cook a favorite dish to perfection through practice and adjustment. It's about taking complex ideas and distilling them into easy-to-follow, personalized action plans that resonate with your life's journey.

Anchoring and reframing in NLP can be as familiar as everyday tasks like setting your morning alarm or arranging your living room. Anchoring is akin to playing your favorite upbeat song to boost your mood. Just as that song is tied to feelings of happiness and can instantly lift your spirits, anchoring links a physical sensation to a desired emotional state you can trigger when needed.

Reframing, on the other hand, is like rearranging furniture in your home to give it a fresh new look. The room isn't changing in size, but your perception of the space shifts. In the same way, reframing helps you look at a problem or a situation from a different angle, providing a new perspective that could reveal solutions and positivity where you might not have seen them before.

These techniques are about gaining control over your automatic responses and viewing your situation in a new light. They're not complex magic tricks but practical, learnable skills that can significantly impact your daily life. By utilizing anchoring and reframing, you can tune the radio of your emotions to your preferred station and repaint the canvas of your experiences, making the ordinary extraordinary.

Let's take a deeper look at the intricate choreography of setting up NLP anchors and the skill of reframing your thoughts.

Establishing Anchors:
- Selecting Your Physical Stimulus: Think of this as choosing a shortcut key on your keyboard for a frequently used action. The physical stimulus could be a touch on your knuckles or a specific hand gesture – a simple, repeatable action.
- Connecting the Anchor to an Emotion: Once you've chosen your 'shortcut key,' you'll need to link it to a desired emotional state. Imagine programming a favorite playlist to this key, so each press floods you with energy or calm, depending on the tune you pick.
- Practice and Habituation: Just as you would rehearse a part in a play until your lines flow naturally, repeatedly activate your anchor during peak moments of the emotional state you wish to trigger. This turns your anchor into a reflex that brings forth the desired feeling on demand.

Executing Reframing Techniques:
- Identifying and Isolating Limiting Beliefs: Begin by pinpointing the 'bugs' in your thought process, much like troubleshooting a glitch on your computer. What narrative is holding you back?
- Crafting the Alternative Narrative: Now, rewrite the script. Replace the 'bug' with a 'feature'—an empowering belief that encourages growth and positivity.
- Commitment to the New Perspective: Like upgrading your phone's operating system, consistently reinforce this new narrative. Over time, this narrative will run 'in the background' of your mind, optimizing your mental framework and enriching your perspective on life's challenges.

These NLP techniques are not just theoretical concepts but are tools as functional and vital as the devices and apps we use every day. They can revamp the way you process experiences and emotions, effectively remastering the soundtrack of your life and renovating the landscape of your inner world.

Oprah Winfrey and Tony Robbins have deftly applied NLP techniques to bolster their communication skills and connect deeply with their audiences. Oprah, with her keen ability to listen and empathize, often mirrors her guests' body language and speech patterns, which is a textbook NLP rapport-building technique. This subtle mimicry helps create a sense of trust and understanding, allowing her guests to open up more fully during interviews.

Tony Robbins, as a life coach, uses language patterns to reshape his clients' thought processes. He often employs the NLP technique of reframing to help individuals reinterpret their experiences in a positive light. By tactfully challenging their narratives, he guides them to discover empowering perspectives on seemingly adverse situations.

Both Oprah and Tony use these NLP strategies not as isolated tools but integrated into their broader skill sets, enhancing their natural abilities to influence and inspire. These methods contribute significantly to their success, proving the practical value of NLP when adopted by skilled practitioners in real-world contexts.

In the office, just as a skilled chef knows the right spices to turn a bland dish into a culinary delight, an adept manager can use NLP techniques to transform a tense meeting into a productive brainstorming session. By using positive language, reframing challenges as opportunities, and mirroring the posture and tone of team members, the manager fosters a collaborative environment where everyone feels heard and valued.

In personal relationships, consider the times when a simple misunderstanding escalates into a conflict. Here, NLP strategies can be as handy as a trusty Swiss Army knife. Active listening to really understand what the other person is saying, and then validating their feelings can de-escalate the situation. Empathetic communication, akin to applying a soothing balm, can help both parties feel understood and pave the way toward resolution.

NLP's value lies in these practical, everyday applications. It isn't about manipulating conversations but about enriching connections—whether that's making sure a friend feels supported during tough times, or ensuring a colleague knows their contributions are appreciated. The toolbox that NLP provides is full of such instruments; ones that accentuate the harmonics of human interaction and make the music of our relationships more melodious.

Here's the breakdown of the NLP reframing process used to resolve conflicts, much like following a recipe to bake a harmonious conversation pie:

- **Identification of Conflict Triggers**:
  - **Recognizing Communication Breakdowns**:
  - Look for accusatory language that assigns blame, similar to spotting burnt edges on a pie crust - it's a sign something's amiss.
  - Notice raised voices or rapid speech; they're like the kitchen getting too hot, signaling that things are escalating.
  - **Observing Emotional Responses**:
  - Pay attention to defensive body language - crossed arms might indicate a barrier as clearly as a closed oven door.
  - Be aware of interruptions and not listening, similar to missing ingredient cues in a recipe, which leads to an unsatisfying result.

- **Application of Reframing Techniques**:
  - **Actively Listening**:
  - Like measuring ingredients carefully, take in every word without jumping to conclusions to ensure you understand the full flavor of their concerns.
  - **Validating Perspectives**:
  - Acknowledge the other person's feelings as you would taste-test during cooking, confirming you appreciate the flavors they bring to the table.

- **Maintaining Post-Reframing Communication**:
  - **Applying the New Narrative**:
  - Keep using this collaborative communication style regularly, just as you'd stick to a tried-and-true baking technique for consistent, tasty results.
  - **Importance of Mutual Agreement**:
  - Ensure all parties concur with the reframed situation, establishing a clear understanding much like setting the table before a meal to indicate it's ready to be enjoyed.

With these steps, you can cool down heated exchanges and transform sour moments into sweet resolutions. Just as the right approach can turn raw ingredients into a delightful dessert, effective use of reframing can bake antagonism into accord.

Neuro-Linguistic Programming (NLP) stands out as a substantial resource for self-improvement and effective communication, with its real-world applicability across various aspects of daily life. By embracing NLP, individuals can sharpen their ability to navigate complex social interactions, enhance personal relationships, and achieve professional goals with greater clarity and confidence. The strategies and techniques of NLP, grounded in the science of behavior and perception, equip people with the skills needed to reshape thought patterns and elicit positive change. In summation, the practical use of NLP can empower personal transformation and improve the quality of one's interactions and overall life experience.

CONCLUSION

As we reach the conclusion of 'Neuro-Linguistic Programming Made Easy', it's clear that the journey through the intricate world of NLP has been enlightening. We've unraveled the complexities of how our neurology, language, and programming intertwine to shape our experiences and reality. The key themes of self-awareness, communication mastery, and purposeful change have been the guideposts along this enlightening path.

We have delved into the ways our thoughts and words have the power to construct or constrain us and discovered strategies to unlock new potentials. The practical examples and exercises provided have shown how to apply NLP techniques in everyday life, whether that be in forging stronger relationships, achieving career goals, or cultivating a more resilient mindset.

Reflecting on the book's impact, it is evident that the true value of NLP lies in its applicability; its principles act as tools to sculpt the life you desire. NLP is revealed not as a quick fix but as a lifelong companion, offering continual insights and strategies for personal development.

As you set this book aside, consider how the art of reprogramming your linguistic and cognitive patterns can be the catalyst for profound transformation. Contemplate the significance of the phrase "the map is not the territory"; our perceptions are merely interpretations of reality, and we hold the power to redraw the boundaries and chart new courses. The journey of exploring NLP does not end here but rather continues with every interaction and thought. May you carry forward the lessons learned and the NLP skills honed, embracing the endless possibilities that await in your personal and professional growth.

ABOUT THE AUTHOR

Jon Adams brings a wealth of experience from over twenty years in the information technology industry, having worked with some of the world's leading tech giants.

With a deep-seated passion for science, technology, and languages, Jon excels at demystifying complex subjects, making them accessible and engaging to a broad audience.

His writings focus on breaking down intricate topics into everyday terms, helping readers not just learn but also apply this knowledge in their daily lives.Currently,

Jon is a proud member of Green Mountain Computing, which publishes his insightful books. Through his work, he aims to foster a deeper understanding and appreciation of technology and science, enriching readers' lives.

Jon@GreenMountainComputing.com